D1151233

MODERN ALPINE CLIMBING
Equipment and Techniques

*Bergell Alps, SW Switzerland - Climbers on the classic ice climb of the
North face of the Cima di Rosso: Photo: John Cleare*

MODERN
ALPINE CLIMBING
Equipment and Techniques

by

PIT SCHUBERT

Translated by

G Steele & M Vápeníková

CICERONE PRESS
MILNTHORPE, CUMBRIA

© Pit Schubert 1991
ISBN 1 85284 067 6

DIE ANWENDUNG DES SEILES IN FELS UND EIS
First published as
Die Anwendung des Seiles in Fels und Eis
by Bergverlag Rudolf Rother, 1985

TRANSLATOR'S NOTE

In translating this book every effort has been made to retain Pit Schubert's individual style although it has occasionally been necessary to change the description of techniques slightly so as to make them more recognisable to British climbers. No attempt has been made to alter anything which might seem controversial because it was felt that the author's opinions should be paramount.

Front cover:
Gendarme on the Lenzspitze, Pennine Alps
Photo: Brian Cosby

CONTENTS

THE CLIMBING TEAM

Partners in the climbing team should be approximately of equal strength, and their performance should not differ widely. Thus, in the case of an emergency, each of the partners would at any time be able to take over the lead.

On **rock** a two man team is usually the rule. Larger teams should be reserved for special circumstances, some of which are described as follows:

Two man team	Three man team	Four man team
Ideal for longer and more difficult routes e.g. in the Alps and other high mountain areas outside Europe, two man teams are to be recommended as in this way assistance can be given more easily.	Used in guided parties or in the absence of the fourth partner; two ropes are used; the leader is tied onto two ropes, the two seconds following are each tied onto the other end of one of the ropes.	Not recommended being too awkward and not fast enough.

As long as both partners are equally capable the two man team lead alternately. A two man team in which the one member acts as a mere second is less frequent. The first one on the rope, ie the leader, accepts the main responsibility. The same applies to guided parties.

On **ice** a three man team should be chosen in preference to a two man party. This is better for giving assistance or helping with rescue, eg in case of falls into crevasses, etc. Other rope teams are rather unusual as stated below:

Two man team	Three man team	Four man team
For climbing tricky ice faces and mixed routes two man teams are recommended.	Ideal for glacier climbs and ascents of not too difficult ice faces.	Ideal for glacier climbs; when climbing ice faces separation into two two man teams is better.

On ice a distinction must be made between glacier and face ascents. On glaciers the climbers move together, with one team member sent out in front, while in ice face climbing the same procedure applies as in rock climbing.

THE CLIMBING ROPE

All climbing ropes presently available comply with the relevant standards (DIN or UIAA) showing the appropriate information, ie UIAA Label or DIN number. Even so rope breaks have still to be taken into account. Rock edges are the cause of most rope breaks because ropes can still not withstand the pressure of sharp edges. As the quality is improving the danger of rope breaks is now on the decrease.

Coiling the rope

Carrying on the back

Classification -
End marking on UIAA ropes

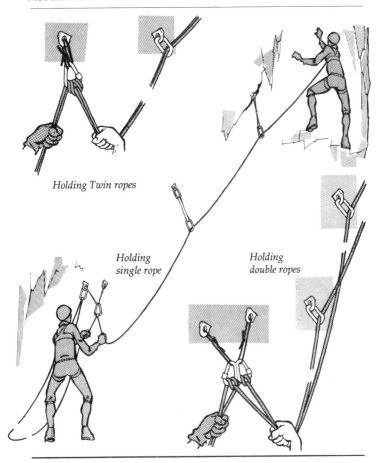

Holding Twin ropes

Holding
single rope

Holding
double ropes

Classification of ropes

According to the relevant standards single and double ropes are
recognised: the standards do not stipulate precise diameters.

Single rope
Band mark 1
Diameter range: approx from 10 to 11.5mm

Used as a single rope.
Only half of the total rope length can be used for abseiling, consequently retreat can pose problems.

Rope for use double
Band mark $1/2$
Diameter range from 8.5 to 9.5mm
Used as a double rope (double rope is two parallel strands of half rope) Abseiling using the whole length of one strand is possible.

Rope performance
The relevant standards stipulate the minimum requirements only. Both ropes, those for use double as well for use single, must resist at least 5 drop tests without breaking, using appropriate testing equipment with one of the two falling blocks and loading over an edge of 5mm radius. Ropes for use double are tested using a block of 55kg and single ropes one of 80kg.

Ropes available for sale differ in performance characteristics, as some manufacturers have improved their products considerably beyond the minimum values set by the standards. Thus the rope which endures the largest number of drops in the test can be considered to be the most likely to survive loading over a rock edge. These ropes (with 9 or more drops) are known as multi drop ropes and have a higher capability when loaded over sharp edges than those which only survive 5 drops in the test.

They have a better chance of resisting sharp rock edges compared with those ropes just meeting the minimum of 5 drops required by the standards.
["Edge resistance" describes the ability of the rope running over a rock edge to bear the force of a fall at the same time.]

The term "multi-drop rope" does not imply that the rope can be exposed to frequent high forces in falls. Every rope should be discarded after a serious fall as its "edge resistance" will have been partly decreased.

All ropes of the "kernmantel" construction are made from polyamide (nylon) fibres. These ropes consist of a core, which is more-or-less bundled up, and a sheath which is woven around the core. The purpose of this sheath is to protect the core and to increase the edge resistance of the rope, ie to give support to the core as well.

There must be no compromise - if the sheath of a kernmantel rope has been damaged, the rope must be discarded.

Useful life of a rope
Climbing ropes are affected by ageing. Until now this field has not been thoroughly investigated. The fact that every rope - even the newest and most durable - can break over a sharp edge, shows that information supplied with the rope may be questionable. For this reason only data based on the tests in the various standards is relevant.

On the whole the useful life of a rope depends on frequency of use, on handling of the rope and on the kind of use to which the rope has previously been exposed, eg holding a fall, towing, etc. At present there are two established clues to assess the useful life which can be expected from a rope.

First, considering present knowledge, but excluding heavy external damage such as rock falls, etc, the typical useful life of a climbing rope depends on the number of drops the rope survived in the tests as shown in the following table:

No of drops survived according to standards (new rope)	Average useful life of rope (does not apply to loading over rock edges)
12 or more	200 hours of use
9 or more	150 hours of use
6 or more	100 hours of use

The second clue depends upon the frequency of use and is even less precise.

Frequency of use	Useful life
Infrequently used (holidays and some weekends)	2 to 3 years
Frequent use (holidays and many weekends)	1 to 2 years
Very frequent (guide or professional climber)	1 summer season to 1 year

The low numbers apply to ropes which just meet the requirements of the standard and the higher to mult-drop ropes.

Longer useful life is also related to weight. Multi-drop ropes (9 or more drops) are somewhat heavier than those which only survive 5 drops. The difference in weight for single ropes is approximately from 15g/m.

	Approx diameter (mm)	Drops survived in test	Weight (g/m)
Rope with 5 drops	10	5	65 - 70
Multi-drop	1.5	12 or more	80 - 85

If the ropes are only used on glaciers their useful life can be doubled or even trebled. On glaciers they are not subjected to sharp edges - but beware on rock ridges and summit rocks.

For twin ropes there is still not enough knowledge about their useful life. Nevertheless it can be expected to be higher than that for a multi-drop single rope.

All textile materials are damaged by the effect of light, in particular by ultraviolet radiation which is especially intense at high altitudes. As to climbing ropes, this effect is quite insignificant, when compared with other potential damaging influences and can be ignored.

Impregnated ropes

Capillary effects mean that ropes can absorb water so that their weight increases by up to 50%. Dampness throughout the rope leads to a decrease in its strength, which is often underestimated.

Wet ropes survive one to three drops less than dry ones. The same applies to iced up ropes, showing the limitation of the standards which only consider dry ropes.

Ropes labelled as 'Everdry' or 'Superdry' are impregnated and consequently absorb less moisture. It is, however, not yet clear to what extent the impregnation decreases during the rope's life.

Length of ropes

All ropes are available in different lengths. Ropes shorter than 40m are NOT viable. The common lengths are 40, 45 and 50m, A length of 40m is often too short for dynamic belaying. The most advantageous is:

> - on rock 45m
> - on ice 50m

All leading rope manufacturers as well as most climbing shops offer ropes in these lengths or can, at least, supply ropes of these length to order.

Care of ropes

Climbing ropes should always be handled carefully. Any trampling on them can cause damage.

As to drying, ropes should be hung loosely in an airy place, not in bright sunlight and not too near any source of heat. Note: too close contact of ropes with car heaters, as well as with chemicals and their fumes may also be damaging. For the proper storage of ropes during longer periods use of a dry but not too warm room is most appropriate. After each mountain tour the rope should be visually examined metre by metre. The sheath is considerably damaged if any spot seems to be fused ie if irregular lumps or changes in diameter occur. Then the rope should be discarded on grounds of safety. Providing that they are not damaged the remnants of this rope can still be used to make slings for larger chocks.

Choosing a rope

To choose the right type of rope several criteria have to be taken into account:

- the terrain (rock, steep ice, glaciers)
- difficulties of the ascent and/or the whole route
- length and location of the route, ie training rock features or high mountains. Such preliminary evaluation could prove very useful should a retreat become necessary
- size of the climbing team: two or three man

On all longer routes and in high mountains, a retreat must be taken into account. Single rope enables retreat by abseiling from one stance to another over only half the maximum pitch length. Double or twin ropes must therefore be used on difficult ground.
The particulars can be specified as follows:

Grade & type of climb	Type of rope	Handling
Two man team on rock		
High mountains: I to IV	Single rope ca 11.5mm dia	As single rope (abseiling only possible over half of pitch length)
Training rocks I to X inc	Multi-drop rope (at least 9 drops)	
Artificial pitches A0 to A4	Two ropes for use double ca 8.5mm dia	As double rope or as twin ropes (abseiling possible full pitch length)
High mountains and training rocks V to X (inc A0 to A4)		

Grade & type of climb	Type of rope	Handling
Three man team on rock		
High mountains and training rocks I to X (inc A0 to A4)	Two single ropes ca 10.5mm dia with at least 5 drops	The leader is attached to the two ropes and the other two are each attached to one end of one of the other ropes.
Two man team on ice		
Belaying on glacier ascents	Single rope ca 10.5 to 11.5mm dia or a rope for use double ca 8.5 to 9.5mm dia	As a single rope On glaciers as a single rope, when climbing a peak with ridges and rock edges, as a twin rope.
Belaying on snow and ice flanks	Single rope ca 10.5 to 11.5mm dia, Or even better, two ropes for use double ca 8.5 to 9.5mm dia	As single rope (abseiling over half of pitch only). As twin rope or, less frequently, double rope (abseiling over full pitch length)

Grade & type of climb	Type of rope	Handling
Three man team on Ice		
Belaying on glacier ascents	Single rope ca 10.5 to 11.5mm dia	As single rope
Belaying on snow ice flanks	Two ropes for use double ca 8.5 to 9.5mm dia	The leader is attached to the two ropes and the other two are each attached to one end of one of the other ropes.
Four man team on ice		
Belaying on glacier ascents	Single rope ca 10.5 to 11.5mm dia	As single rope

OTHER EQUIPMENT FOR ROCK CLIMBING

Accessory cord and Tape slings
It is now possible to buy accessory cords of between 4 and 8 mm diameter meeting standards from DIN or the UIAA . The strength requirements are indicated in the following table. There is no 9 mm diameter accessory cord because of possible confusion with climbing ropes for use double. Less than 4 mm diameter are not considered because of their inadequate strength.

Diameter	Minimum breaking strength (DIN or UIAA)
4mm	3.2kN
5mm	5.0kN
6mm	7.2kN
7mm	9.8kN
8mm	12.8kN

For thicker or stronger slings use climbing rope of either size. The minimum breaking strength can easily be calculated from the following formula:

$$\text{Min breaking strength (kN)} = \frac{d^2 \text{ (mm)}}{5}$$

eg. 5mm dia accessory cord

$$\text{Min breaking strength} = \frac{5^2}{5} = 5\text{kN}$$

Accessory cord is basically the same as kernmantel climbing rope so it is also necessary to discard it when the sheath shows any signs of

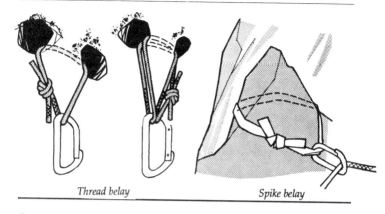

Thread belay   *Spike belay*

damage. The most useful length is approx 1.8 meters tied with a tape knot or a double fisherman's knot. Such a length can be carried over the shoulder. Ensure that the ends outside the knots are at least as long in cm as the diameter is in mm.

It is now possible to buy tape material meeting DIN and UIAA standards. Various widths and thicknesses are available but since July 1986 tape has been produced with stripes of a distinctive colour so as to indicate the strength which can be expected. Each stripe indicates 5kN. The breaking strengths are therefore according to the following table:

No of Stripes	Minimum breaking strength (DIN or UIAA)
1	5kN
2	10kN
3	15kN
4	20kN

Tape has a higher resistance when loaded over a rock edge than that demonstrated by accessory cord.

Always tie tape slings with the tape knot as other knots pull apart under load. Ensure that enough tape is left outside the knots, a minimum of 3 times the width is recommended.

Express slings are short sewn slings made from tape. DIN and UIAA have appropriate standards. The minimum breaking strength is 22kN. The stitching must be in a contrasting colour and should be checked from time to time for wear and tear. They are used as extension slings on running belays.

The requirements for an typical rock or ice route are:

- 2 accessory cord slings for prusiking (6mm dia, length 1.8m);
- one accessory cord or tape sling for use forming a triangle between two anchors or for use on rock spikes (8mm dia or 25mm width, 1.8m long);
- several shorter accessory cord slings (5 to 7mm dia) and tape slings (from 15mm width);
- for rock routes several Express slings from 10 to 20 cm long.

Harnesses

Standards have been produced by DIN and UIAA. Harnesses spread the maximum impact force in a fall and after a fall they support the chest, pelvis and thighs during any subsequent period of hanging. That way the maximum impact force is mainly taken on the thighs and pelvis while the chest harness keeps the body upright.

Three different types of harness are available:

- two part harnesses, chest harness and sit harness, they are separate but used together;
- one piece harnesses called full body harnesses.

All harnesses are either adjustable or available in different sizes. When purchasing it is necessary to bear in mind the clothing which might be worn with the harness. Choice is as follows:

- for rock climbing figure of eight shaped chest harness and sit harness, chosen to give the best compromise between weight and comfort when wearing, falling or hanging;
- for ski mountaineering or glacier tours, full body harness

with leg loop which can be unbuckled to allow easy putting on and taking off when wearing skis or crampons, with thicker clothing the leg loops can be adjusted.

Correct choice and adjusting is best done during a hanging test in the shop (a length of rope and a stable fixing on the ceiling can be expected). All harnesses meeting the standards are supplied with instructions for use in which it is obvious how to attach the harness to the rope. See also page 69.

Tying on to a non-approved harness should be done only in an emergency because, although it might withstand a fall, the effect of the impact force or the subsequent hanging could cause fatal injuries. The following are hidden dangers:

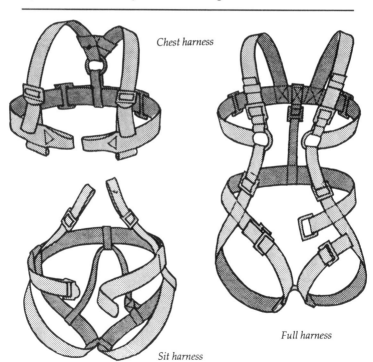

Chest harness

Full harness

Sit harness

- Restriction of the blood vessels when wearing only a chest harness or only a rope around the chest. Within a few seconds(!) unbearable pain occurs which can lead after a short time to circulatory failure.
- Slipping out of the harness when only a chest or only a sit harness is worn.
- Risk of spinal injuries by tipping backwards when only a sit harness is worn.

Karabiners

Standards have been produced by DIN and UIAA. With the gate closed the minimum breaking strength in the major axis is 20kN which is adequate for all practical loads. In poor placement the gate can press against rock or ice and open, resulting in a reduced breaking force between 6 to 9kN and the risk of readily breaking with quite short falls. Therefore karabiners should be so placed, perhaps using extension slings, as to avoid the possibility of the gate opening when the karabiner is under load from pulling or in a fall.

Karabiners with cross gates give a wider opening and can be clipped into awkwardly placed pitons.

Karabiners with curved gates have more disadvantages than advantages. The gate opening is bigger but during a fall it is possible for the the gate to open under quite a light pressure which can allow the rope to come out. This pressure could come from the rope falling across the gate from the outside. Use extension sling to allow the karabiner more freedom of movement.

Karabiners with locking gates (Screw gate karabiners) prevent unwanted opening of the gate. The locking device does not increase the breaking strength.

HMS karabiners (Italian hitch karabiner) is a pear-shaped screw gate karabiner for use with the Italian hitch belay. For protecting the person climbing one of these karabiners is necessary for each member of the roped party. With other karabiners (also with klettersteig karabiners) there is a likelihood of the hitch jamming .

The belaying angle (see diagram) is for the separate use of two HMS karabiners for protecting two simultaneous seconds.

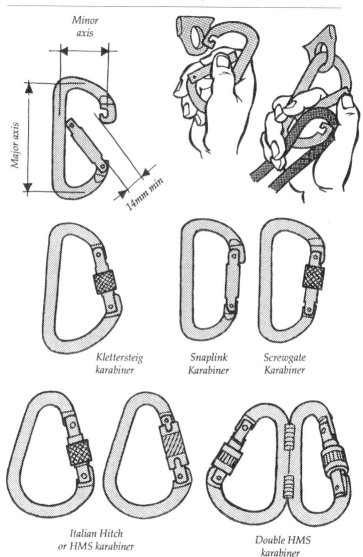

Minor axis

Major axis

14mm min

Klettersteig karabiner

Snaplink Karabiner

Screwgate Karabiner

Italian Hitch or HMS karabiner

Double HMS karabiner

The following numbers of normal karabiners are needed:

On ice	Karabiners per roped party
for glacier ascents for snow and ice flanks for steep ice	approx 5 - 6 approx 8 - 10 approx 10 - 15 (and even more)
On rock	
Difficulty grade I - II Difficulty grade III - IV Difficulty grade V and beyond	approx 3 - 5 approx 8 - 10 approx 15 - 25 (and even more)

Klettersteig karabiners with locking gate and large gate opening are used for security on klettersteig climbs (vie ferratae) where fixed wires, steel pins, steel eyes, ladders, etc. prevent the use of normal karabiners. (These climbs are found particularly in the Dolomites and Austro-German limestone ranges.)

Chocks
They are used as attachment points on rock. It is usually possible to fix them easily and quickly but often they can only be removed with difficulty. It is easier with a chock tool.

Chocks are normally used in cracks which taper downwards allowing them to resist a load in the downward direction. Safe placement so as to resist the forces involved in a fall require careful handling and experience.

All chocks are useable in at least two different directions (length and width) all types are available in different sizes which are numbered. The numbering systems differ between manufacturers and are not comparable one with another. All smaller sizes are provided with wire slings for easier insertion into narrow cracks. Larger chocks are provided with holes for the threading of accessory cord, tape or rope slings.

Brass chocks have a double tapered form and a wire sling the ends of which are soldered so as to fit narrow cracks of perhaps only a few millimetres width. They have a low breaking strength and are not suitable for the forces involved in a large fall, rather just for progress.

'Stoppers' have a double tapered wedge shape. Suitable for narrow cracks.

'Rocks' have a double tapered form curved like a banana. Rocks jam better in cracks because they have larger contact surfaces. The wire sling is very flexible so that it is not necessary to use an extension sling. Available also with holes for threading accessory cord, tape or rope slings.

'Wall nuts' are of a similar shape to 'Rocks' but have concavities in their curved faces and a flexible wire sling. The have many placement possibilities and are the most versatile chock.

'Hexentrics' have irregular hexagonal shapes to provide different chocks widths.

Clog 'Coggers' are irregular hexagonal in shape with all faces and edges rounded. Weight and holding strength are about 10% higher than for hexentrics.

'Camlocks' have a shape similar to a sector of a circle with the curved surface having a rising cam and transverse ridges to improve the grip in cracks. Of advantage in very irregular cracks (limestone) and rock holes.

Chocks with stiff wire slings can be dislodged by movement of the rope (climbing past or flicking rope). Therefore an extension sling of accessory cord or tape must be used. This increases the possible fall length by double the length of the sling.

For maximum safety, chocks with holes for accessory cord, tape or rope slings must be fitted with the strongest sling which will fit the holes. If the sling is too long it is possible to shorten it with an overhand knot. Thereby the possible fall length is reduced.

As a rule there are many more possibilities to place chocks safely than is generally assumed. Well placed chocks can reach holding strengths as high as well placed pitons. Up until now there is no standard for chocks (work is underway). At the moment it is necessary to refer to catalogues for information on holding forces. The highest values are reached by sizes in the middle of the range and are dependent upon the strength of the sling.

Knotted slings are used today only in place of chocks. Because of the flexibility of such knots they are only suitable in cracks where the knot cannot pull through. Use the largest possible knot so as to reduce the chance of it pulling through.

Instead of chocks, chockstones can be used but they should always be checked with several blows of the piton hammer to ensure that they are secure. The threaded slings should not be too thin (rock edges) and should be placed between the chock and the side of the crack.

Adjustable chocks

They are used as attachment points on rock. They are fully adjustable between their largest and smallest sizes. They set automatically to the width of a crack by their spring mechanism. They work in cracks with parallel sides, the cracks need not narrow in the direction of loading as required by chocks. They work as long as there is sufficient friction between the device and the crack walls. Three different types are in use:

- Friends, with 4 movable segments connected by a fixed pin, are the most frequently used adjustable chocks.
- Joker with 3 movable segments connected by a flexible wire cable; ideal for horizontal cracks because the cable adjusts itself into the direction of loading.
- Sliders with 2 wedges which can slide together for use in cracks of finger width.

Safe placement so as to resist the forces involved in a fall require careful handling and experience.

- The rock must be dry and free of sand, earth and lichen.
- all movable segments must be in contact with the rock, otherwise the loading will be one-sided and the device will pull out.

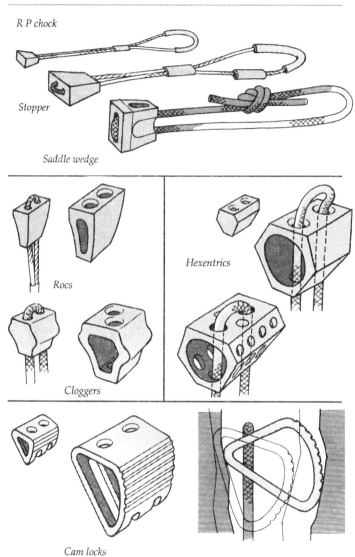

R P chock

Stopper

Saddle wedge

Rocs

Hexentrics

Cloggers

Cam locks

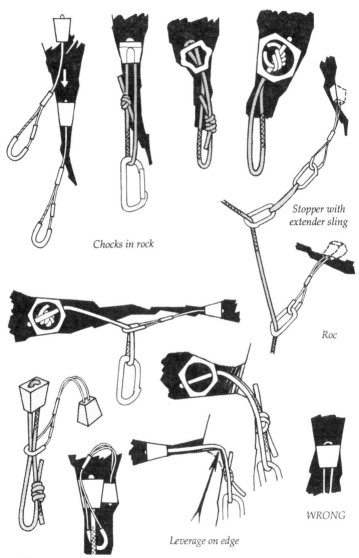

Chocks in rock

Stopper with
extender sling

Roc

Leverage on edge

WRONG

30

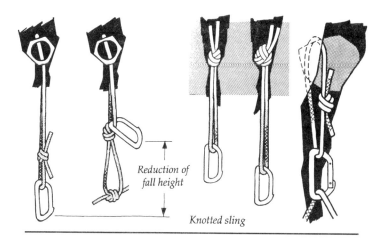

Reduction of fall height

Knotted sling

- surface contact between the segments and the rock must be as large as possible, the segments should not hang only on small protrusions on the rock.
- only about 90% of the width range should be used so as to allow the other 10% for deformation of the material or the rock under load.

Rock Pitons

They are used as anchor points on rock and as progression points in aid climbing. The shaft is driven into rock cracks and the shape and material must be appropriate to the type of rock and the shape of the crack.

Vertical and horizontal pitons are the basic types. The horizontal pitons are more versatile than the vertical ones and they are easier to remove.

Universal pitons with the head at 45° to the blade hold much better in cracks because of the enforced twisting effect. They are more difficult to remove.

Ring pitons are normally used as abseil pitons. The welded ring (which is not tested) is a safety risk.

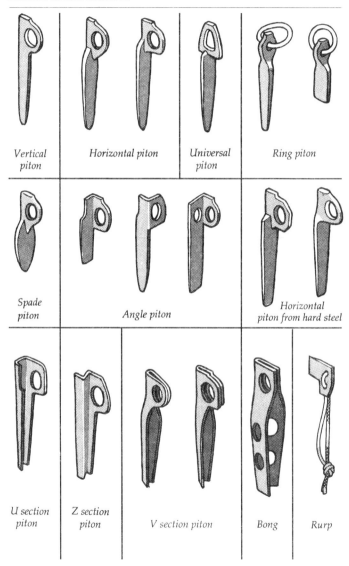

Vertical
piton

Horizontal piton

Universal
piton

Ring piton

Spade
piton

Angle piton

Horizontal
piton from hard steel

U section
piton

Z section
piton

V section piton

Bong

Rurp

Short horizontal pitons (Ace of spades) are for shallow cracks and have only a low holding power.

Lightweight pitons are a simplified form of the horizontal piton as they bend easily when driven. They are only available in short lengths (as Ace of Spades) and for use in shallow cracks.

Channel pitons are used in wider cracks. "U" shaped are for finger-wide cracks and "V" shaped for wider ones. "Bongs" are used in fist-sized cracks.

"Z" Profile pitons are for use in softer rock such as sandstone.

Rurp miniature pitons are used for hollow crack lines in granite (not suitable for limestone because of the risk of splitting the rock). As they will not withstand high loads they are only used for progression.

All pitons are available in various lengths for cracks of differing depths. Pitons with slim sharp points drive better than those with broad points.

Piton Material

There is a difference between hard and soft steels. Soft steel is a tough forging steel, but hard steel is hardened and has a higher strength. The holding force in rock of a hard steel piton is higher than that of a soft steel one. Soft steel pitons are likely to bend under load and will come out easier (like a bent nail) than hard steel ones. Hard steel pegs hold better in cracks than soft steel ones.

Choice of Pitons

Pitons for use on a climb are chosen against various criteria:

type of rock	length of climb
grade of difficulty	frequency of use
use of other anchoring devices (chocks, etc)	

The following information can be used as a guide:

Limestone and soft rock such as sandstone	$2/3$	soft steel
	$1/3$	hard steel
Granite and other hard rock	$1/3$	soft steel
	$2/3$	hard steel

Rigid horizontal pitons, all hard steel horizontal pitons and profile pitons of all types are advantageous. Ring pitons are not usually necessary (limited use) and this also generally applies to vertical pitons. Blade lengths usually from 8 to 11 cm - only a few shorter ones are recommended (easily removed).

The use of pitons is declining in favour of various types of chocks. Pitons are to be preferred only for stances, descent and such places where otherwise only very small chocks (low holding force) could be used.

With increasing difficulty and increasing pitch lengths it is advisable to take more pitons. With increasing frequency of ascents climbs require less pitons. As before it possible to offer rough guidance:

Popular climbs	2 to 3 pitons per climber for emergency plus chocks
Less frequented routes	3 to 6 pitons per climber, plus chocks
Seldom climbed routes	use own experience

The low numbers apply for shorter routes the higher for longer ones.

Piton Hammer

It is used for driving in pitons. It should be purchased with the following criteria in mind:

-   the weight should be not less than 650gm; lighter models are available (500gm). The heavier version is preferred because of its greater impact energy.
-   the length of the shaft should be not less than 27cm; shorter shafts can cause finger injuries on sharp edged rocks.
-   metal shaft with non-slip rubber grip and a hole in the end of the shaft. This is for securing the hammer with approx 1m of thin line, the other end of which is attached to the climbing harness.

Hammer Holster

The best way to carry a piton hammer is in a holster. Carrying in trouser pockets or in a hammer loop is not recommended because damage can occur to the clothing.

Piton Carriers

Used in conjunction with thin accessory cord, a piton carrier can protect against losing a piton by dropping if it is being put in or taken out one-handed. If a carrier is not available the function can still be provided using accessory cord through the eye of the piton.

Driving Pitons

It should be possible to partly insert the piton in the crack by hand (only thus is it possible to drive one-handed). The depth of insertion depends upon the type of rock (harder or softer) and the material of the piton (hard or soft steel) as follows:

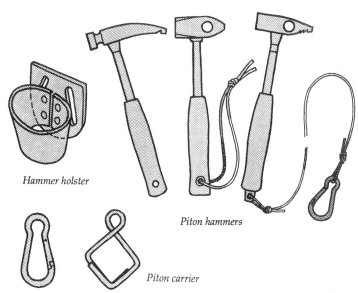

Hammer holster

Piton hammers

Piton carrier

Rock/piton material	Insertion depth (before driving)
Limestone / soft steel pitons }	approx ⅓rd of blade length
Metamorphic rock / hard steel pitons }	approx ⅔rd of blade length

Driving by hammer normally gives adequate security. All pitons are driven into the rock up to the eye. This is done with vigorous blows of the hammer: anyone who is gentle with the hammer cannot expect the piton to hold. The harder a piton is driven the better it will hold.

The depth and width of the crack can be identified with the first few blows of the hammer as follows:

- if the first few blows are well placed and the piton goes in steadily with each blow, then it has been well chosen with regard to length and thickness.
- if the piton eye touches the rock after only a few blows then it is too thin or too short. A longer, thicker piton must be chosen.

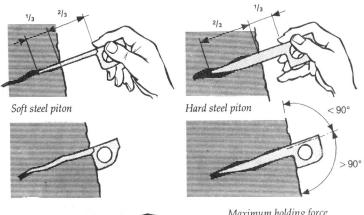

Soft steel piton

Hard steel piton

$< 90°$

$> 90°$

Maximum holding force with angles as shown

Piton cross-section in crack

- if on the other hand several vigorous blows fail to drive the piton up to the eye then it is either too long or too thick. A shorter, thinner piton must be chosen.
- it is always better to drive in a shorter piton up to the eye. A longer piton, protruding from the crack, may wobble if loaded.

After driving a piton check for any widening of the crack due to loosening or flaking of rock around the piton. This will be revealed by 'dull' sounds when tapping the rock.

Holding Strength of Pitons

Due to variations in the nature of rock structures it is not possible to be precise about holding forces. Correct placement of pitons in good rock is a pre-requisite for optimum security. The following values must therefore be considered as rough guidelines only:

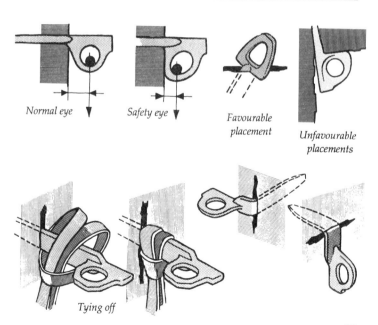

Normal eye   *Safety eye*   *Favourable placement*   *Unfavourable placements*

Tying off

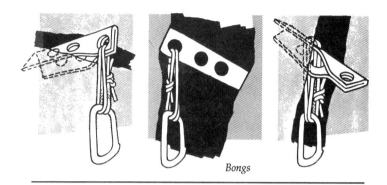

Bongs

Hard steel pitons in vertical cracks	up to 10kN
Hard steel pitons in horizontal cracks	up to 15kN
Soft steel pitons in vertical cracks	up to 4kN
Soft steel pitons in horizontal cracks	up to 8kN

In general higher holding forces can be achieved on granite than on limestone.

The longer the blade the greater the holding force in rock. For anchors on stances pitons should be at least 10cm long. If it is not possible to place a safe anchor (or a chock or thread) then several pitons should be used with blades of not less than 8cm.

The holding force of pitons found already in place is usually over estimated. Corrosion and frost always reduce the holding force. A few cautious blows of the hammer will demonstrate the condition of the piton. A dull or 'loose' sound indicates an unsafe condition, a higher 'singing' points to a safe piton. If the eye is not against the rock a few addition blows of the hammer may help. If even this does not work then the piton must be replaced with a longer and/or thicker blade.

Removal of Pitons
Removal of the piton is achieved by alternate blows to either side of the head in the line of the crack. Soft steel pitons loosen gradually

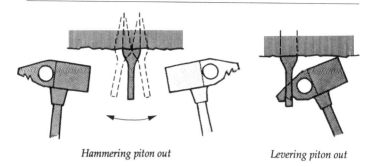

Hammering piton out   *Levering piton out*

with each blow. Hard steel pitons can come out suddenly with a blow. The use of a piton carrier is recommended.

Bolts

They can be fixed in any place providing that the rock is solid or firm. A self drilling bolt is driven into the rock whilst being continually turned. The direction of the hole should, if possible, slope downwards a little. Using the wedge the bolt is locked into position. Bolts are used either with welded rings or with a threaded hole into which a hanger can be fixed using a screw. The thread is subject to corrosion therefore sealing is essential. Breaking strength when

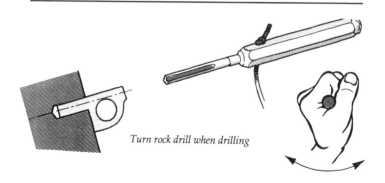

Turn rock drill when drilling

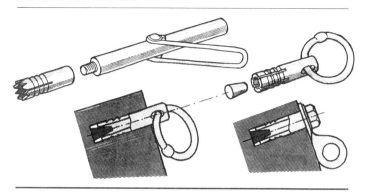

new (not after corrosion) is approx 20kN. This applies only for industrial bolts not for DIY pitons.

Étriers

There are étriers on the market made from aluminium steps and accessory cord or even from tape, all are fitted with Fiffi hooks. Unfortunately they are rarely the right size, in relation to the climber's build, for length, number of, and distance between, steps. It is therefore recommended to make one's own. Metal steps are available in climbing shops.

The following bits are needed for making one étrier:

-   3 or 4 metal steps
-   5mm diameter accessory cord. Approx 4m for height of 1.70m (5¹/₂ft). For other heights, more or less in proportion.
-   one Fiffi hook or Griff-Fiffi hook.

Length of the étrier should be such that, with the Fiffi hook at shoulder height, one can step into the lowest rung with the leg bent. The distance between the steps should decrease with the increasing height of the étrier. If 2 étriers are to be used the accessory cords should be of different colours. This will reduce the risk of a tangle.

Tape étriers, sewn from flat tape material are available in the shops.

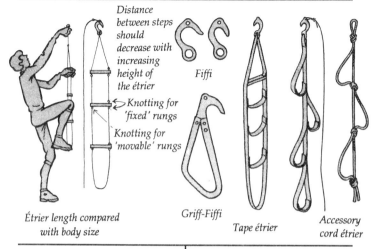

Distance between steps should decrease with increasing height of the étrier

Fiffi

Knotting for 'fixed' rungs

Knotting for 'movable' rungs

Étrier length compared with body size

Griff-Fiffi

Tape étrier

Accessory cord étrier

Ascenders

They take over the function of a Prusik knot and allow ascent of the rope with less effort. Two different sizes are available:

- ascenders with a handle for gripping (about 250gm weight) mainly used for ascent of fixed ropes when 2 ascenders are required.
- without a handle (weight about 160gm) mainly for self belay with a top rope (see page 81).

Securing the ascender on the rope is done automatically by means of clamps with a spring mechanism. A locking catch prevents

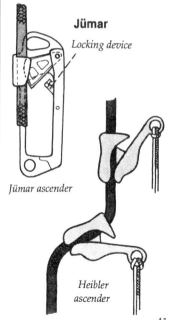

Jümar

Locking device

Jümar ascender

Heibler ascender

the rope coming out unintentionally during use. Pay attention to the manufacturer's recommended strength. Should be at least 4kN.

Figure of Eight
Made from aluminium (from 80 to 130gm) they are used for abseiling. Easy to use.

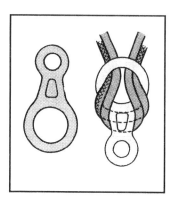

Bent Figure of Eight
These provide 2 different levels of friction, one for double rope and the other for single rope, whereas With the normal type, movement of the braking hand produces the different braking force. According to manufacturers claims the strength is 20kN or more. Forces of this magnitude do not occur in use. The maximum is about 3 times body weight or about 3kN.

OTHER EQUIPMENT FOR ICE

Ice tools

They are distinguished according to:

- shape especially of the pick and the remaining parts (adze or hammer) and
- shaft length (normal ice axes are the longest, technical ice axes and hammers the shortest).

The shape of the pick and the length of the shaft depend upon the purpose for which the equipment is intended, if the ice axe is intended for cutting steps for the leader or hanging on during progression up steep ice:

Used for cutting steps for the leader	slightly curved pick (dimension A is larger than dimension B) with adze and shaft length 70 - 95cm.
Used for hanging on during progression up	steeply curved or bent pick (dimension A is smaller than steep ice dimension B) with adze or hammer and shaft length 35 - 70cm.

Ice equipment with a curved pick , dimension A is approx the same as dimension B, are suitable - even if not ideally - for both cutting steps and also for a buried axe anchor.

The pick should have teeth on the lower edge. The inner curve at the base of the teeth must be smoothly rounded (otherwise there is an increased risk of breaking due to impact). Teeth on the upper edge are a disadvantage (additional risk of breaking and more difficult to remove from the ice).

The toothed area of the pick should be free of stampings such as

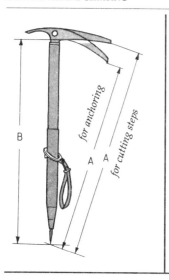

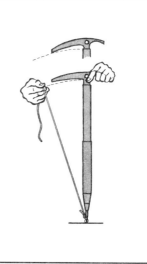

for anchoring

for cutting steps

B

A A

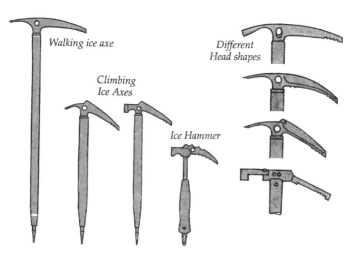

Walking ice axe

Different
Head shapes

Climbing
Ice Axes

Ice Hammer

manufacturer's trade marks or model name as this could lead to a risk of breakage at this point.

Normal ice axes are available with shaft lengths 55 - 95cm. When used as a leader axe on glacier tours the length should be related the the user's height. When standing upright with the axe hanging loosely from the hand at the side, its point should just touch the ground. When used for hanging on during progression up steep ice it advisable to have a somewhat shorter length (larger moment).

Technical ice axes are available with shaft lengths 45 - 60cm. Some have a hammer for use with ice pitons.

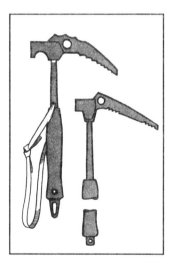

Ice hammers are available with shaft lengths 35 - 45cm. The longer models have a spike at the end of the shaft (similar to ice axes of both types) so that the differences between technical ice axes and ice hammers becomes blurred.

The strength of the shaft especially the head attachnent and the security of the spike are covered in a standard. For protection (against cold or bruising) the shaft is covered with a insulating and energy absorbing sleeve. The better the protection the less force is required to strike into the ice.

Modular ice axes

All leading manufacturers offer ice tools with interchangeable picks, adzes and hammer heads. This allows the use of picks of different shapes and broken parts can be replaced (there is, as yet no standard for the strength of the picks). Most systems are still not fully developed (there is no logical coupling between the interchangeable parts, which can loosen in use). Changing the parts requires special tools and a vice may be required. At present the only recommended system, which can be changed in the field (glacier, steep ice) without difficulty, is the model Tyrol from Stubai.

Choice of ice tools
The choice depends upon the intended use and the likely terrain.

Used for cutting steps for the leader and probing glaciers	Slightly curved pick (dimension A is larger than dimension B) with adze and shaft length 70 - 95cm depending upon height.
Used for cutting out stances and for fixing ice pitons as well as for climbing ice slopes of up to 60°	Two ice tools, one with an adze the other with a hammer. Both with steeply curved or bent picks (dimension A is smaller than dimension B). The shaft lengths will be different, the tool with the adze 60 - 70cm and that with a hammer 35 - 55cm.
As immediately above but for climbing extremely steep ice (60° to vertical) on alpine ice walls and frozen waterfalls	Three tools, one with adze, two with hammers, (the second hammer is used as a replacement in case the adze is broken). Shape of the pick and shaft length as immediately above, shaft lengths of the spare tool approx 35cm (ice hammer); in place of the third tool a spare pick can be carried such as from the Stubai model Tyrol.

Securing the ice axe

For securing the leader's ice axe there are two standard methods:

- wrist loop and sliding ring
- accessory cord sling or narrow tape sling

Wrist loops are suitable for glacier tours and less steep snow climbs where the axe is mainly used in one hand. Also useful in an emergency (ice axe braking) as the ice axe head is still near to hand should it be lost during a slip.

An accessory cord or tape sling, fastened through the hole in the head of the axe, and attached to the harness is more suitable for steeper glacier routes and for ridges where the axe must be changed frequently from one hand to the other. A wrist loop here would be a hindrance.

When ice tools are used for hanging on during progression on steep ice the wrist loop serves to relieve the strain on fingers and hand muscles. Its length must be precisely adjusted. If possible it must be fastened in only one shaft hole to avoid fluttering of the sling during striking. For easier handling and as a protection against slipping, the wrist loop should have an adjuster to reduce its size more nearly to that of the wrist.

*Axe shaft
with wrist sling*

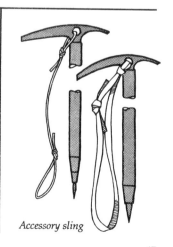

Accessory sling

Ice axe brake

The pick can be used in case of a fall as a brake. This necessitates holding the axe in the hand so as to be ready, that is with the pick pointing backwards.

A fall can have many variations. The braking procedure should be as follows:

- arms and legs should be spread so as to stabilise the position of the body and to prevent rotation and tumbling.
- turn the body to face downwards.
- keep crampons away from the slope (they easily catch and cause rotation and tumbling as well as injuries).
- use the feet for braking only when not wearing crampons.
- with the ice axe in both hands push the pick into the snow as deep as possible.

Crampons

There are five different types generally available (weights between 500 and 1000 gm). The choice is made according to the intended use as follows:

- lightweight crampons for use on easy ice or snow terrain but when full crampons are not justified (question of weight).
- universal crampons, with an articulated joint, suitable for use on ice and glacier tours, also on mixed terrain (ice and rocks) and steep ice up to 60°.
- crampons for extreme ice which give a better standing position because of the second of the two pairs of forward facing points. Also suitable for glacier tours but not for mixed terrain.
- rigid crampons for extreme ice and mixed climbing (Chouniard-rigid crampon) offering a safe position even in the steepest and hardest ice. Because of the special shape of the front points they are also suitable for short stretches of rock climbing. A disadvantage is that there is a strong possibilty of 'balling-up'. A layer of plastic sheet underneath the boot can reduce his problem.

49

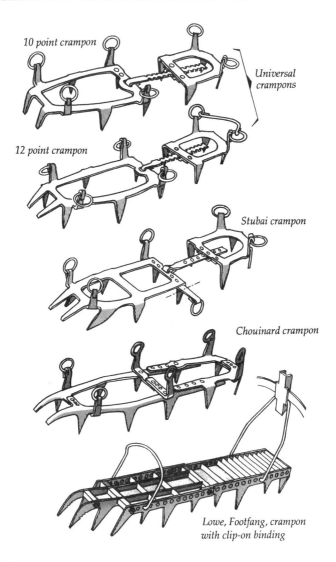

10 point crampon

Universal crampons

12 point crampon

Stubai crampon

Chouinard crampon

Lowe, Footfang, crampon
with clip-on binding

- rigid crampons in a box form for extreme ice (Lowe Footfang crampons) because of the three pairs of front points a good standing position is offered. Unsuitable for mixed climbing or walking on glaciers, only for steep ice.

All crampons are available in an adjustable form. Ensure that they are a good fit. The crampon should fit snugly, and without movement, between the binding posts. All crampons will be used occasionally in mixed terrain and the points will eventually be blunted. Sharpen with a file.

For fastening on the boots choose either strap bindings or a clip-on binding. The differences are as follows:

- The earlier strap bindings are not now much used and have disadvantages. There is a high possibility of restricting the blood circulation and causing frostbite.
- Clip-on bindings (to tighten on the heel) avoid this. Plastic boots allow a better grip than leather boots because the latter do not always have an adequate welt (depending on the boot shape and sole stiffness).

Use of vertical points

For less steep ice. Feet are put in such a way, that all vertical points grip at the same time. This requires - according to steepness of the slope - large or smaller twist at the ankle. Pay attention to the following points ;

- regardless of the slope the body must always be upright.
- the feet should be in a slightly open 'V' (too large a 'V' position can cause overbalancing).
- distance between the feet at least one good foot width.
- on steeper passages use ice axe (hold in hand nearer to ice).

Front point technique

Front point technique is used for straight ascent and descent on steeper firn (snow-ice) and ice slopes.(approx. 45 deg). Two ice axes or ice hammers (or one of each) are necessary for progression and for maintenance of body balance.

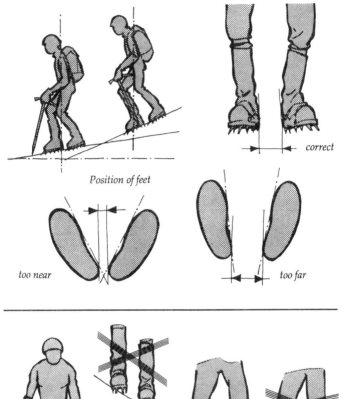

Position of feet

correct

too near

too far

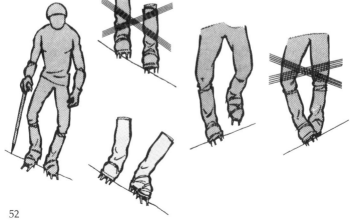

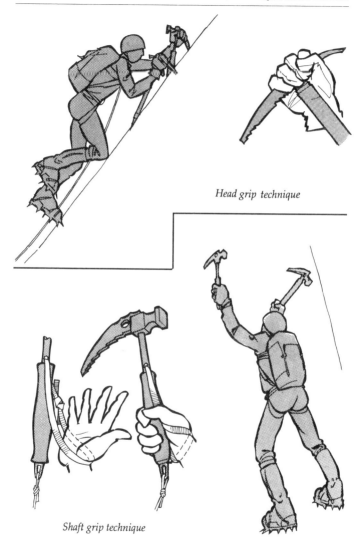

Head grip technique

Shaft grip technique

'Four footed" technique

Caterpillar technique

Leg technique
- Using a vigorous swinging action with the lower leg the front pairs of points, and also the first pair of vertical points, will penetrate the ice.
- application of this force brings about a shift of balance, so the heel should be kept low. (Standing is easier and less tiring than hanging on the arms.)

Technique with hands

- use head grip technique on firn as well as on soft, less steep ice. This means that the hand is on the ice axe head. In this way the axe can be removed more easily from the ice.
- shaft grip technique is to be used on hard and steep ice. The shaft is held allowing the axe to be swung which results in a deeper and more secure penetration into the ice.

Choice of technique depends upon the steepness and type of ice:

- firn and soft, less steep ice, 'feline' technique (right arm/left leg/left arm/right leg). On less steep ground the movement can proceed as follows : the right arm/left leg move simultaneously , followed by simultaneous movement of the left arm/right leg. On steeper terrain, preference should be given to separate movements of arms and legs.
- hard and steep ice : 'shuffle technique' - right arm/left arm (reach about 50cm), afterwards right leg/left leg (stepping height 50cm).Consecutive movements only.

'Combi-technique'
Long stretches of front point technique on steep firn and ice slopes

55

is always strenuous, especially at high altitude.

It is possible to combine one foot on front points and the other on all points to give easier progression and resting. This is called 'combi technique'. It is also useful when descending or retreating. In ascent both four-legged (feline) or 'shuffle' techniques can be used. In descent only the shuffle technique should be used. (see diagrams)

'Combi-technique' allows the possibility to master both techniques at the same time. Using them alternately is recommended: front point technique with the left leg then, later, vice versa.

Ice screws and ice pitons

These are used as anchor points on ice. As a result of numerous programmes by the DAV Safety Circle it is now known which ice screws and types of new ice piton have sufficient holding power. The minimum holding force is 10kN.

- only screws and pitons of tubular form penetrate the ice without fracturing it and provide the necessary performance. The larger the diameter the better the holding power in ice.

- all other types of screws and pitons - e.g. semi-tubular or solid, cork screw, conical shape (including spiral pitons - 'drive in screw out') - are not advisable as their holding power is often well below 10kN. In addition conical ice screws and ice pitons, and all solid versions split or fracture the ice instead of giving good penetration.

Tubular ice screws and tubular ice pitons are usually available in various lengths. To achieve the minimum holding power of 10kN, a minimum effective length is required. (This recommended length is not the total length but that part of the ice screw or ice piton which is screwed or driven in.)

The minimum effective lengths of ice screws and ice pitons should be 15cm and 18cm respectively.

Shorter ice screws and ice pitons are used for thin ice layers on rock, and their holding power is correspondingly lower. Longer ice screws and ice pitons, such as of 25cm effective length, are not necessary.

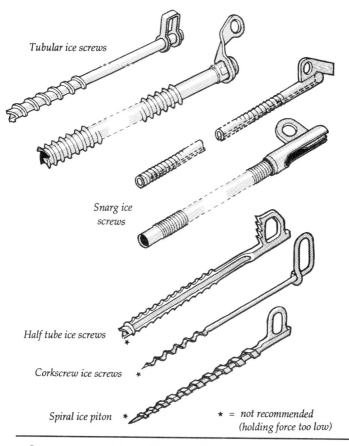

Tubular ice screws

Snarg ice
screws

Half tube ice screws ★

Corkscrew ice screws ★

Spiral ice piton ★   ★ = *not recommended
(holding force too low)*

Ice screws and ice pitons of aluminium or titanium are recommended because of their low weight.

As ice pitons are driven in the ice refreezes around them faster than with ice screws which must be screwed in. Ice pitons are best used as running belays which can be fixed quickly, and also as the first anchor point at the stance. As the second fixing point at the stance an ice screw is recommended.

The required numbers of ice screws and ice pitons

- For glacier walking/climbing: two ice screws per rope party are required in emergency.
- Climbing on ice walls up to 55° (of steepness), two tubular ice screws and three tubular ice pitons per rope party are advisable (one ice screw and one ice peg on each stance, three ice pitons as running belays).
- It is advisable to take additional tubular ice pitons as well as several tubular ice screws for steeper ice climbs (more runners). These numbers also depend on the ability of the climbers.

Setting of ice screws and ice pitons
Any brittle ice on the surface is cut out until firm ice appears.
    All tubular ice screws as well as all tubular ice pitons should be

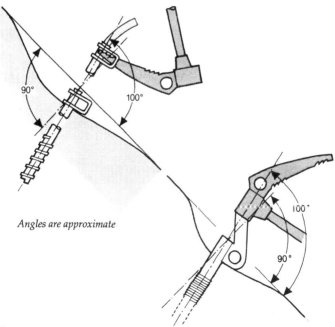

Angles are approximate

at an angle of 100° with the ice surface - this is a lower setting angle jokingly referred to as '90° plus a bit more'.

By means of a few hammer blows tubular ice screws are driven into the ice, until resistance is obvious (in emergency an ice axe may be used). It is then screwed into the ice using the pick of the ice hammer (or with another ice screw or an ice peg) until the eye is pointing downwards and set firmly in the ice. Only ice screws with an extra sharp cutting crown can be set without the initial driving in.

Tubular ice pitons are driven into ice with vigorous hammer blows until the eye is sitting on the ice firmly. During the driving in the tubular ice peg is revolving slightly around its longitudinal axis (thread). It is therefore the best to start with the eye at '20 minutes past the hour'.

Tubular ice screws and tubular ice pitons are removed by unscrewing (twisting out). The first two or three revolutions may need the use of an ice tool but screws and pitons can mostly be unscrewed by hand. After removal the ice plug must be removed. The screw or peg may need to be warmed up in the hand and the plug extracted by knocking out, or - if not needed again immediately - it should be hung on the climbing harness; the plug will then slowly melt and come out.

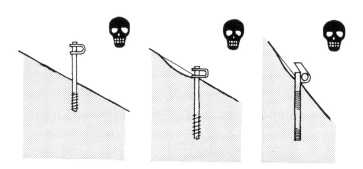

Dead Man Snow Anchor

Its use is controversial. When under load, it may dig itself deeper into the snow, thus withstanding the fall load, but it may just as well break loose. Criteria for safe stability on snow are still not known.

On principle, use of dead man anchors has to be discouraged. it is better to use the buried ice axe anchor instead.

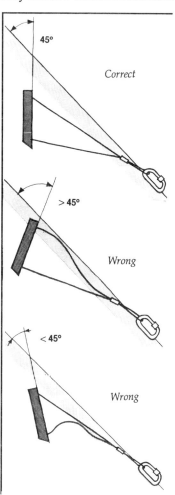

If, in spite of the afore-mentioned, dead man anchors are used, then at least the following rules have to be observed in order not to affect the anchor's stability from the very beginning:

-   The aluminium plate must be angled in shape (rather than flat).
-   The steel cable must come down from the aluminium plate at less than a certain angle to prevent it coming out of the snow.
-   The anchor must be set into the snow at an angle of approximately 45°.
-   The dead man anchor should be pushed into the snow as deep as possible.
-   The snow should be packed down above the anchor and in the likely direction of the anchor's movement.

Even if the dead man anchor withstands the load, it is always very time consuming to take it out, as it may be up to one metre deep in the snow.

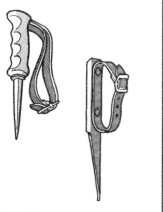

Ice-fiffi
Just as a fiffi is used with rock pitons on rock, an ice fifi can also be used on ice. This device may then be coupled with an étrier or tape sling, for artificial climbing. With an accessory rope, the ice fiffi can be used as a sitting fiffi when resting, and together with a hand loop, as an ice tool for ascent on steep ice. The impact momentum can be increased by adding screwed-in weights as produced by Salewa.

Snow shovel
A snow shovel can be fixed to a walking or climbing ice axe or an ice hammer. It has a whole variety of uses. It can be used not only as optimum support for both ascent and descent on steep snow slopes, but also for digging in case of rescue, or for digging of snow caves and snow holes.

Because of its versatility, it is advisable to always take a snow shovel along on ice tours.

Pulleys and rollers

Pulleys and rollers (the latter hung in a karabiner), are used to reduce the troublesome rope friction during a rescue from a crevasse. There are various models on the market, but only those with movable brackets are recommended as this type facilitates putting the rope in.

KNOTS

Let's concentrate on mastering the following knots which are sufficient in all practical situations. The following points should be observed:

- It must always be possible to tie knots safely even in the dark and under the pressure of time.
- After the knots have been tied they must always be tightened immediately. The end must not be too short: both climbing rope ends and slings' ends must not be less in cm than rope diameters are in mm. Length on the tape ends must be not less than three times the tape width.

Tensile loads cause weakening of all textile fibres in the knots. Relative knot strengths can be expressed as the ratio of ultimate load in the knotted rope to the ultimate load of the rope without knots. Relative knot strengths vary between 50% and 70% depending on the type of knot and the diameter and make of the rope. Relative strength is only relevant to accessory cord and tape. It is less

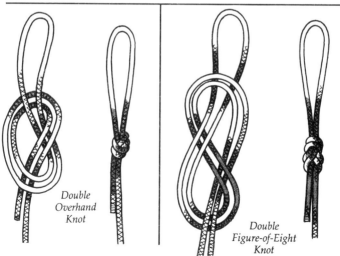

Double
Overhand
Knot

Double
Figure-of-Eight
Knot

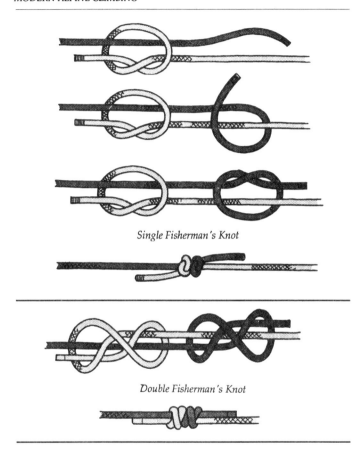

Single Fisherman's Knot

Double Fisherman's Knot

relevant to climbing ropes, which are now so designed that they are unlikely to break in the knots even at the maximum load.

Locking knots
(Locking knots are usually tied in an accessory cord around the climbing rope.) After being tied round a fixed rope locking knots tighten under load. They can, however, be moved when the load is

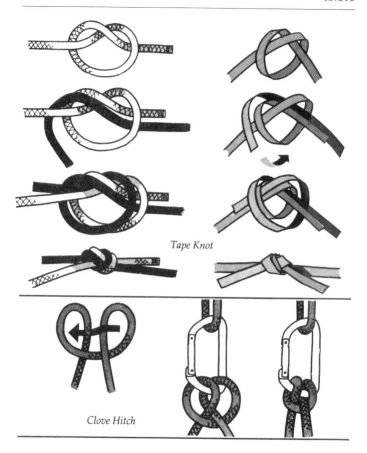

Tape Knot

Clove Hitch

removed from the accessory cord.

There must be a certain ratio between the diameter of the accessory cord and that of the rope otherwise there is no locking effect. As a rule the accessory cord should be half the diameter of the rope.

If both climbing rope and accessory cord are wet or ice up, then extra turn must be taken in each knot.

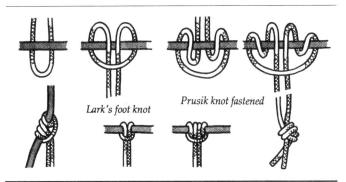

Lark's foot knot

Prusik knot fastened

Locking knots are used as follows:

- for ascending a fixed rope, Prusik knot, other locking knot or double rope locking device. (see p.67)
- for pulley systems, Prusik knot, Bachmann knot.
- for self-security during abseiling, Prusik knot.

When 5mm accessory cord is used, all locking knots may be used regardless of rope type, i.e. single rope, half rope or twin rope (two parallel half ropes). If, however, only thicker accessory cord is available, one extra turn must be taken as with all diameters if wet or iced up.

The double rope locking device (from Salewa) makes tying of locking knots much easier but it has no other use.

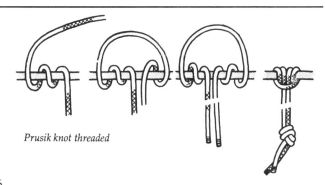

Prusik knot threaded

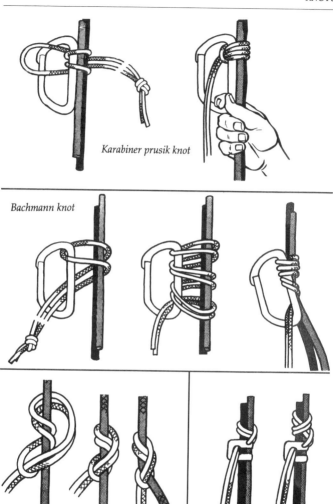

Karabiner prusik knot

Bachmann knot

Locking knot

Double rope
locking device

THE USE OF THE ROPE FOR BELAYING ON ROCK

Roping up alone will not guarantee safety in the event of a fall. Only the correct application of a belaying method can protect a falling climber or the fall of a complete roped party.

Even a properly applied belaying method, which reduces the length of the fall, cannot prevent impact or abrasion against the rock which can cause serious or even fatal injuries. The length of a fall depends upon the amount of slack, stretch of the rope and run through in the dynamic belay. The effect is that the fall length is about 2.5 times the distance from the last running belay.

Not every running belay whether chock, Friend or rock piton is able to withstand the force developed in the fall. If any is pulled out this increases the fall length and the risk of injury. The only answer is to climb safely and well within one's capabilities. Dangerous moves should only be made when a runner is close at hand.

When moving together there is always the danger of the whole party falling. The rope transfers the force from one end to the other and does not prevent a fall.

Therefore any member of the party must at any time be able to protect the others or himself. This is done by belaying the other members or by self belay. The differences are as follows:

- 	belaying the other members, protecting them against falls
- 	self belay, protecting oneself against a fall.

Both methods take place on the stance. Protecting members of the party with a body belay is prone to danger. For details see:

- 	establishing the stance (page 71)
- 	self belay (page 81)
- 	belaying other members of the party (page 84)

Roping up on rock
The following has to be born in mind when putting on the harness (chest harness and sit harness or full harness).

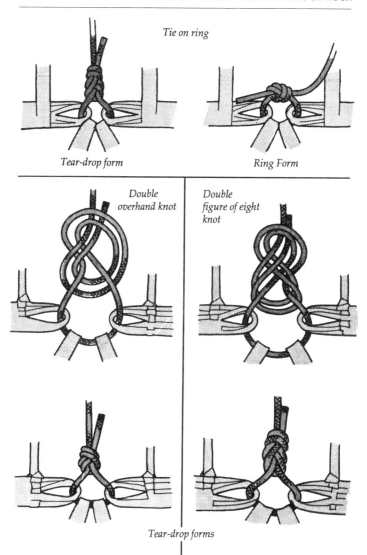

Tie on ring

Tear-drop form

Ring Form

Double overhand knot

Double figure of eight knot

Tear-drop forms

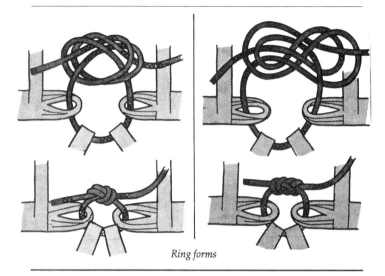

Ring forms

- the chest harness has to be chosen or adjusted in such a way that the rope attachment loops have a gap of 2 - 3 finger breadths. (Too small a gap is unnecessarily tight around the upper part of the body and can cause breathing difficulties if hanging free.)

- the chest harness should be put on 2 hand's breadth below the arm pits, the rope attachment loops will be somewhat lower at the front and the chest harness somewhat higher at the back.

- the sit harness has to be chosen or adjusted in such a way that it cannot slip over the hips during climbers' normal movement. The correct fit of a harness or combination of chest and sit harness can be found out only by hanging in it. The best method of tying on depends on the kind of sit harness:

- When a two part harness is used follow the above diagrams.

- Use of the sit harness shown on page 23 gives a better roping up method. The chest harness can be taken off when clothing is changed without untying the self-belay.

The best knots for tying on are either the double overhead knot or the double figure of 8 knot. (The latter is somewhat bulkier but easier to untie after a fall.)

Roping up by means of twin rope
Only the double overhand knot is of use. The double figure of 8 knot is too bulky with twin ropes. There are two methods from which to choose.

- to tie each single rope separately allowing the possibility when necessary to untie one rope without untying the knot of the other rope. ·
- to tie up both ropes parallel with one knot and put each rope end through one of the rope attachment loops and joining the two ropes with the tape knot or single fisherman's knot
- in this way the roping up is less bulky.

Setting up the stance
On the stance a sufficiently safe fixed point must be available, or must be established for anchoring the non-climbing members or the party. Without a secure anchor the stance cannot be used to belay members of the party. The following may be used to provide the secure anchor:

- rock pitons
- fixed or adjustable chocks (placed so as to withstand the pull from the most likely direction)

Loading possible in all directions

Correct

Wrong
Sling lifts off with a pull

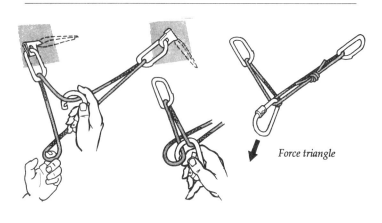

Force triangle

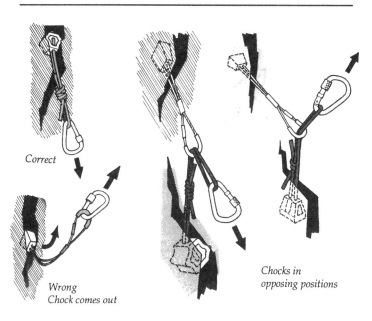

Correct

*Wrong
Chock comes out*

*Chocks in
opposing positions*

- thread belays
- rock spikes or flakes - load only down not upwards
- trees

Ideally it must be possible to load the anchor point in all the likely directions according to the climbing situations which may mean downwards, upwards or sideways.

If an anchor can be loaded in one direction only (many chocks, wedges, spikes) but the force from a fall may come from another direction, then a second anchor point must be established to cover the other pull direction(s). Both anchor points should be braced against each other with a sling.

If one anchor appears not to be safe enough then a second one must be placed so as to form a central anchor point by way of the force triangle from the two separate ones. Attention must be paid to the following:

- to choose anchors as close as possible to each other so as not to create too large a triangle. (Otherwise when inverted by an upward pull significant extension of the fall length may occur.) If a large force triangle cannot be avoided it should be secured by a third anchor to resist an upward pull.
- the angle should not exceed 90°. (Otherwise there is no useful force distribution.)

If anchors are found on the stances, checks must be made to ensure their security or safe fit. This is a matter for visual inspection and judgement, in the case of pitons tapping on them with the hammer. If the existing anchors do not seem safe enough then alternatives should be sought. With pitons it often helps to drive them in deeper.

The survival of the whole rope party depends on the security of the anchor points on the stance.

Italian hitch belay - single rope
Only pear-shaped karabiners (marked 'HMS) are suitable. Normal karabiners (D-shaped) have a tendency to block the rope.

The HMS karabiner should not be hung directly in a piton or

Italian hitch with single rope

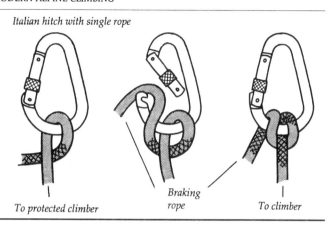

To protected climber   *Braking rope*   To climber

wired sling (chock) but attached by means of a short rope or tape sling (min 7mm dia or tape of at least 15kN strength, 3 marker threads, and of length ca 1m untied). This sling ensures freedom of movement of the belaying karabiner against all possible direction of pull in the event of a fall. When using multiple anchors, rope or tape slings, a thread or spike anchor, no further sling is required.

Operating the Italian hitch (paying out and taking in the rope) is done with one hand on the rope on either side of the karabiner. The hand nearest the climber is referred to as the guiding hand and the other one is the braking hand. Between paying out and taking in the rope, and vice versa, the knot actually reverses as it is pulled through the karabiner from one side to the other.

If the climber falls, the rope must be held firmly by vigorous action of the braking hand. (This must become an instinctive action.) In the case of a long fall and higher fall factor the rope will run through the Italian hitch karabiner at speed. More than about $\frac{1}{2}$ metre of run-through brings the risk of burns to the braking hand. This can be prevented by using a belaying glove, preferably with a leather palm.

There is no difference in the action of the Italian hitch between belaying the leader and belaying the second, the procedure is

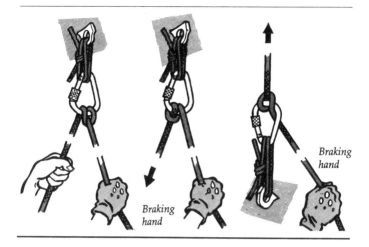

always the same.

Anchoring of the belayer with karabiner and clove hitch or double overhand knot can take place directly onto the same anchor point as used for the belay, but the use of separate anchor points is the safest method.

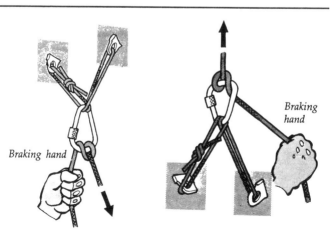

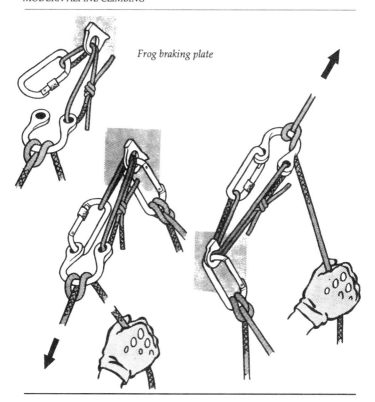

Frog braking plate

Italian hitch belay - twin rope

Both ropes are handled in parallel, i.e. they are handled as a single rope thus

- clip both ropes in all running belays (the rope should run in as straight a line as possible). If necessary use extension slings (express slings).
- use both ropes together in the HMS karabiner to provide the Italian hitch belay.

Advantage: For descent or retreat there are two ropes available, so that the full rope length can be used in an abseil.

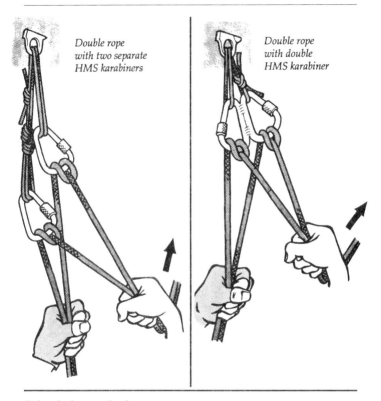

Double rope with two separate HMS karabiners

Double rope with double HMS karabiner

Other belay methods

Belay techniques explained below are also occasionally used. Their shortcomings can be first summarised as follows:

- the braking forces which can be achieved are not of the correct order of magnitude.
- the braking action in both pull directions (upward and downward) needs different manipulation.
- in the case of an upward pull the braking force is higher than in the case of the downward one, (the reverse would be much better).

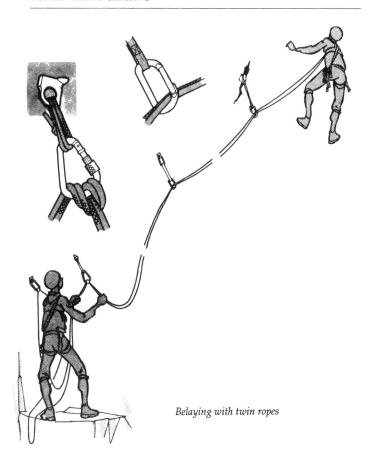

Belaying with twin ropes

- perfect operation of the belay at the anchor point is not assured.
- perfect operation is not guaranteed solely by an instinctive action.

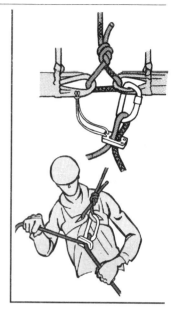

Sticht belay plate

The braking action is achieved by means of a slotted plate through which the rope runs, and returns, via a karabiner. Different slot sizes are used for the two major rope diameters. The Sticht belay is operated with one hand on the rope running to, and one from, the device. To operate, the braking hand must be pulled upward (not an instinctive action). A higher braking force can be achieved if another karabiner is hung alongside (parallel with) the first one and the rope threaded through both.

Disadvantages: This type of belay requires consideration of the rope diameter and the number of ropes. Different braking forces can be achieved only by careful manipulation or by using two, instead of one, karabiners. Perfect operation is not guaranteed by an instinctive action. This belay method can only be properly used when attached to the body of the belayer.

Karabiner cross belay

The rope is passed through two karabiners attached to the chest harness. One or more half twists are put into the two strands of the rope to provide the necessary friction to brake the fall. The braking force depends on the number of half twists in the rope. Paying out or taking in is done with either hand.

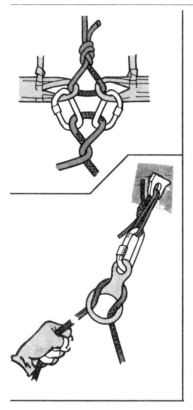

Disadvantages: Undefined braking force. Braking force can only be varied through altering the number of half twists in the rope (one more or less). Judging the correct number of twists is difficult, as the shape can change under load (in the event of a fall) when compared with the unloaded state. Braking force with a downward pull is less than with an upward one (the opposite would be better). Only possible to use on the body.

Belay with a figure of 8
Braking effect is the same as when abseiling. Paying out or taking in is possible with either hand.

Disadvantages: In the case of a downward pull the braking force is much too low (lower than when abseiling and there is extensive rope run-through leading to a significant increase in the fall distance. Burning of the belaying hand can occur even with small falls.

Top rope belay
This type of belay is used for practising, maximum length of climb = $^1/_2$ rope used = one rope length. The climber is belayed by one of the partners on the ground using an anchor suitable for an upward

pull (piton, chock, thread belay, etc).

At the top the rope must run through a karabiner which should hang free of the rock. Only in this way can the rope be handled with the minimum of friction against the rock. Attention! Under no circumstances must a rope or tape sling be used without a karabiner otherwise the effect of the rope running through the sling during taking in or lowering will be to melt the sling leading to breakage (numerous accidents have been caused in this manner).

Belaying is by Italian hitch belay or by figure of 8 held close to the body, the most suitable attachment to the belayer being the loop where the rope is tied to the sit harness. This is justifiable as there is no possibility of a significant fall length. In addition much friction is produced where the rope passes through the karabiner at the top. While belaying the following has to be borne in mind:

- The belayer should not be substantially different in weight to the climber (maximum difference about 10kg) otherwise the belayer may be lifted up (danger of the rope running out of control).
- The belayer should not stand too far from the fall line (certainly not so as to create an angle of more than 30° in the line of the rock face) otherwise the belayer may be pulled off his feet towards the rock (danger of the rope running out of control).

Self-belay with top rope

This method is used when climbing routes of a length not more than the length of the rope.

The rope is anchored safely at the top (pitons, chocks, tree, etc.) and should not run over sharp rock edges. Where it lies on the ground, a small weight should be put on it (approx. from 1 to 2kg, small rucksack, strong tree bough, etc.) In this way, movement of the ascenders is facilitated.

The climber belays himself with one ascender such as a Jumar (the small Petzl ascender, size B8 is the most suitable, while the Hiebler clamp is less suitable).

The ascender is fastened to the sit harness. Attention should be

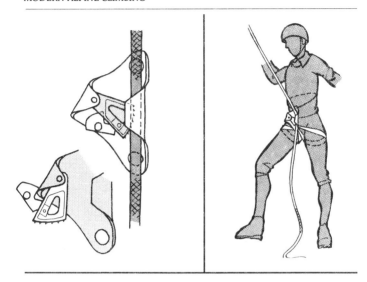

paid to ensure that the ascender is in a vertical position on the rope. After the ascender has been attached to the rope, the lock should be applied (most ascenders have an automatic spring mechanism for this purpose).

Before climbing, the correct application of the system should be checked, by jumping on it. Be careful to ensure that the ascent is more or less vertical. Do not attempt anything which will result in an extreme pendulum fall!

During climbing the ascender slides up the rope. In the event of a fall the device will lock onto the rope. Warning! Free fall is to be avoided, as there is the danger of possibly breaking the clamp (there should be no significant slack rope above the climber).

Small weights to keep rope tight

MOVEMENT OF THE ROPED PARTY ON ROCK

If climbers are roped together, climbing and belaying should be done in a properly organised fashion. Simultaneous movement does not offer safety as there is always the danger of a fall involving the whole party. A fall by one member of the group means that the others are dragged along. The load is transferred from one end of the rope to the other.

Two-man roped team
There is always only one person climbing, belayed by his anchored partner.

Movement
of
two man team

Three-man roped team

Only some members of the team are climbing, either the leader or the two followers.

The leader is belayed by only one of the followers on twin rope (if they belay on one rope each, the forces in the belay chain are doubled in the event of a fall). The twin rope is placed in each running belay.

Having reached the stance, the leader belays the two followers who climb simultaneously, but with a short distance between them so that they do not obstruct each other. Warning! If the first follower falls, the rope will stretch by approximately 10%. It is therefore advisable to keep a separation initally of at least 5m, later less; if the rope is slack correspondingly more.

Movement of three man team

Belaying climber

Non-belaying climber

Ropes should be taken out of runners as followers:

The first of the two followers

- takes both ropes out, when the pitch is vertical or almost vertical;
- when the pitch is diagonal or horizontal (pendulum fall), only his rope is taken out.

Braking reserve

When belaying the leader, the second on the rope, or the person belaying in the three-man roped party, must keep approximately 5m of rope in reserve. This reserve is necessary for a dynamic belay to operate with longer falls. If, in order to reach the next stance, the braking reserve must also be used, it is advisable to place at least one reliable running belay so as to restrict the length of a fall at this point of the pitch. By reducing the fall length the energy of the fall can be held on a static belay. The fall factor is reduced (approx. 0.2) and the forces generated are well within the capabilities of the Italian hitch belay. This happens without putting too heavy a load on the belay chain.

Good rope management

Pulling the rope along requires a certain effort because of its weight and the friction of the rope in running belays and on rock edges. As well as requiring unnecessary effort, the rope is damaged by stronger friction, and makes climbing more difficult. The rope or twin rope should glide through all karabiners and over all rock edges as smoothly as possible.

The lowest friction in the karabiner is achieved if the karabiner makes a right angle with the rock, without being affected by external forces, and if the karabiner's inside opening is crosswise towards the lay of the rope. This can be achieved by using a second karabiner, an express sling or a rope or tape sling, which act like a universal joint.

By using slings, the karabiners are to be placed in such a way that in the event of a fall

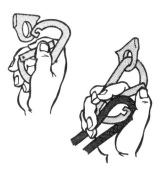

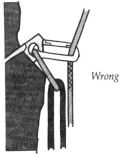

Wrong

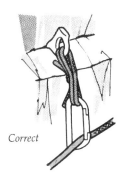

Correct

- they are not subjected to bending load (otherwise there is a danger of breaking);
- the gate cannot open itself by contact with the rock (otherwise there is a danger of breaking);
- there is no danger of the rope jamming on the rock (otherwise dynamic belay is impossible).

The rope run within a pitch should be as straight as possible (any deviation from the straight line leads to higher rope friction). It is therefore advisable to extend unfavourably placed running belays by express slings, belay rope slings or tape slings. However, in the event of a fall, this extension can lead to an increase in fall length. The extension should therefore not be larger than absolutely necessary:

- straight rope run: no extension
- rope deviating a little: short extension slings (approximately from 10 to 15cm)
- rope deviation at larger angles: only on such places should longer slings be used.

87

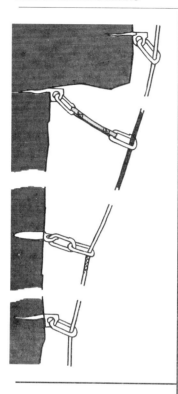

Doubled sling holds better than single loop

In an emergency return to the nearest running belay and reduce rope friction (by extending or clipping out). In aid climbing (climbing with help of pegs), individual progression pegs can be unclipped after passing, preferably those which appear unstable.

Slings on rock spikes may be detached when the rope is above. A specially placed sling will prevent it.

Communications between climbers

They should be brief and clear. Negative commands such as "Do not pull" should be avoided. The first word is often suppressed by wind or overheard by the partner (during the first phase of listening), who may then respond in a wrong way. Members of a roped party should therefore use straightforward commands only.

There are the following commands used within one pitch:

- the belayer informs the leader, about the amount of rope left, eg "Still 10m, 5m, all up", without indicating the braking

The less the rope friction in karabiners and on the rock, the easier the climbing

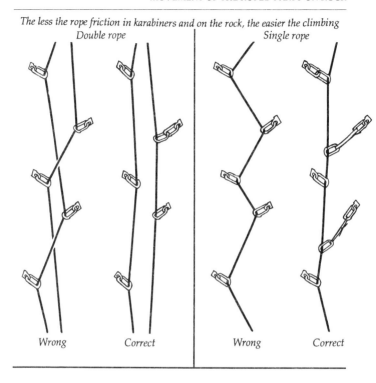

Double rope		Single rope	
Wrong	*Correct*	*Wrong*	*Correct*

reserve (ca. 5 m) (assuming a 45 metre-rope is used)

- With the rope still available the leader tries to find a stance and to fix his anchor. Only then is the second informed by a call: "Belayed" or "Safe".
- The second now releases the leader's belay and the leader takes in the remaining metres of the rope. If the rope is all taken in, the following information is given by the second to the first one: "That is me".
- The leader then belays the second using the rope, while informing him by a call: "Climb when you are ready". The second unfastens his anchor and starts to climb.

When assistance is required from the rope during climbing, the following command is given: "Tight rope". The end this assistance is announced by a command: "Stop pulling". In case of slack in the rope, the command is: "Take in slack". If double rope is used, the corresponding colour must be announced clearly, eg "Take in on red" or "Slack on yellow".

Choice and change of stance

If there is no convenient stance to be found within the last few metres of rope, it will be necessary to return to a previous one. If this is not possible either, a poor stance must be arranged on steep rock, or even a hanging stance in slings. At the beginning of a pitch an attempt should be made to locate a likely next stance. Occasionally a stance has to be occupied after 20 metres or less in order to avoid an uncomfortable stance in slings.

If several pitches in succession are led by one member of the party (not leading through), the climbers must change places on the stance. This must happen only in such way that, at any time, everybody is anchored. The procedure is as follows:

- Having arrived at the stance, the second will establish his own anchor, while being still belayed by the leader.
- Only then is the belay of the second released.

10 metres left

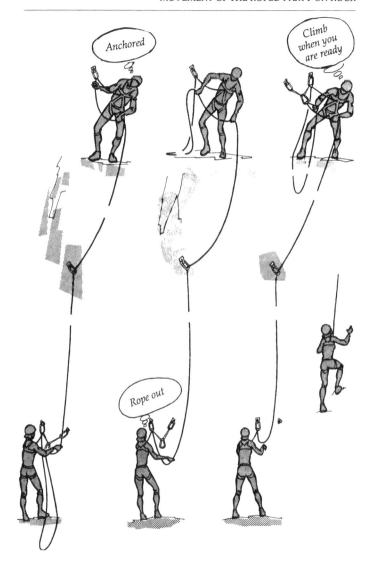

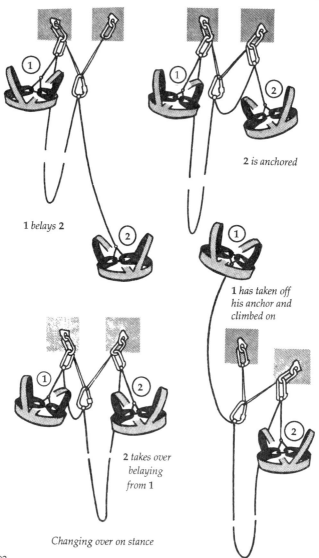

1 belays 2

2 is anchored

1 has taken off
his anchor and
climbed on

2 takes over
belaying
from 1

Changing over on stance

- The belay of the leader is taken over by the second.
- Only then can the leader untie his own anchor and continue with the climb.

If the climbers lead through, no change at the stance is required. The second climber, while passing the first one, takes over the leadership. The partner's belay does not require any change. This belay continues smoothly.

If leading through and change over on the stance are not advisable because of peculiarities of the stance, the second will occupy any suitable stance within the pitch and the leader will carry on with the next pitch.

FREE CLIMBING

This is climbing without using artificial aids to progress. Only the rock with its variety of holds is used for hands and feet: pegs, chocks, etc., are used only for running belays or anchors.

Differences in rock formations require climbing techniques adjusted to the particular type of rock. The following methods are distinguished:

- climbing cracks as wide as a finger, hand, fist or shoulder;
- chimney climbing (bridging or back-and-footing);
- climbing corners;
- climbing walls/faces;
- climbing slabs.

Other kinds of climbing are:

- steep and overhanging wall techniques (hanging and using hands for moving upwards;
- bridging technique.

The rock with its variety of structures requires frequent changes of the various techniques of free climbing.

There is virtually no climbing which can be accomplished by using a continuous sequence of short arm pulls. As conditioned by nature, feet and legs are stronger than arms and hands. Body weight should therefore be borne largely by the legs, the arms being used to keep one's balance. Only in case of more difficult passages, where support by the legs is less possible, must the larger proportion of effort be taken over by the arms.

To maintain balance safely it is advisable to have three points of contact on the rock, either both feet and one hand. or both hands and one foot. The remaining hand or foot can be used to make the next hold or step, or for checking the solidity of the rock (Three-point-rule). On difficult climbing sections the main load must often be borne by two points of contact only - those are as a rule one hand and one foot - while the climber can gain partial support from the other foot and/or the other hand.

Crack climbing

Laybacking

Corner climbing

Bridging

Wall climbing

Straddling

Traversing

Back & foot

Chimney climbing

Slab climbing

AID CLIMBING

Even though the route might have been chosen within the participants' climbing capabilities, it can sometimes become impossible to progress by means of free climbing. To avoid retreat artificial aids may have to be used.

Even if the climber resorts to pitons only he does not climb freely any more but in an artificial way, using piton techniques.

In emergency situations (such as injury, pressure of time, sudden worsening in weather conditions, etc.), artificial aids can be used to make progress.

Free climbing is at present considered to be of great significance, giving the climber a special and meaningful experience. Nevertheless, the overcoming of large overhanging rocks and roofs, with artificial aids, brings about an experience of exposure, which is very impressive and exciting. An alpine climber probably gets the greatest enjoyment from routes in which the majority of climbing is free but in which some artificial sections are involved.

As in other cases, so also with aid climbing: all physical movements should be as efficient as possible and undue exertion should be avoided, especially early in the climb. Even on a very steep face or cliff, the main part of the body weight should as often as possible be shifted to the feet. From time immemorial man has been holding himself upright and, consequently, his legs have developed stronger than his arms. The latter get tired faster than the former.

The use of ropes for direct assistance in traverses may also be classified as artificial climbing, even if the rest of the route has been accomplished by free climbing. The traverses may be tackled with a tight rope, with a fixed rope or as a pendulum; all described later.

Self assistance
To hold the piton firmly requires strength. Use of the rope passed through a karabiner in the piton makes it easier. After the rope has

Leader

Second

been clipped into the karabiner, the leader raises himself by pulling the rope while the belayer takes in the slack. Thus, it is relatively easy to hang on a piton with only one hand. The higher the climber moves, the greater the load on the piton (the outward pull). This danger is reduced by using étriers.

The second can also assist himself by pulling on the rope as described above. In this case the belayed leader takes in the slack. It is impractical to use a separate rope for self assistance because of the time taken threading it through pitons or karabiners.

Climbing with étriers

For most climbs one étrier used together with a self pulling technique is sufficient. Another étrier is taken along only in case of more difficult or longer routes, mainly in the Western Alps, where the leader is also carrying a rucksack.

- The fiffi hook is hung in the piton's karabiner by the leader.

Resting in étriers

Height gained

This is the easiest way to recover the étrier. A few centimetres of height may be gained if the fiffi hook is hung in the piton eye, but it frequently jams and pulling it up is difficult.

- The second man always hangs the fiffi hook in the piton eye. This can make it difficult to remove the karabiner. Such difficulty can be avoided, however, if the karabiner is removed prior to hanging the fiffi hook in the piton.

Hooking the front of the heel on the rung is the best position for safe standing in an étrier.

Rope traverse with a single rope
Rope assistance may be used for short traverses, without holds or steps, where setting up a fixed rope could be too complicated.

- During the traverse, the required rope is paid out to the leader by his anchored second after receiving an appropriate request from the leader.

99

Tension traverse with single rope

The leader leans firmly against the pull using friction. He tries as much as possible to avoid losing height, and uses whatever holds or purchase he can find in order to reach ground which can be climbed freely again.

- The second man has to use an adequately long length of accessory cord which has been passed through a piton. This belay cord is removed after the traverse has been completed.

Rope traverse with twin rope

When using twin ropes, the leader and the second can give themselves assistance from the rope. This way the climbers can better maintain balance when on a traverse with scarce holds.

- For this purpose one of the two ropes is used by the leader whilst being belayed on the other rope by the second.
- The second uses one of the two ropes to provide a loop of the appropriate length. If the piton eye is not large enough, a short

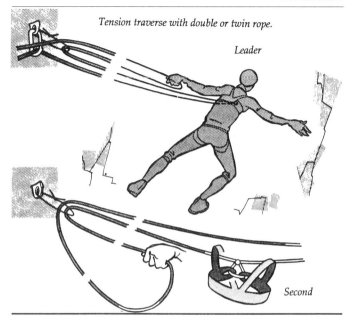

Tension traverse with double or twin rope.

Leader

Second

length of accessory cord must be tied (into the piton eye). The other rope is used by the leader to belay the second.

- When the second has also reached rock suitable for free climbing, the rope loop is removed, the accessory cord loop, however, is left behind.

Rope traverse with fixed rope
If a traverse is unsuitable for free climbing and its length does not allow use of rope assistance and/or self pull, then a fixed rope is used. For this purpose, a second rope is required which is used by the leader for making a sideways abseil, and by the second as a fixed rope.

- At the start of the traverse a safe piton is fixed as high as possible. Just as in the case of abseiling, tying off with a short length of accessory cord makes it easier to remove the rope

Fixing and using

later. The leader abseils across in the traverse direction using
a figure of eight.

- During the sideways abseil the leader leans against the rope
  in the direction of the traverse. The abseil rope is handled in
  just the same way as it would be in abseiling. With one of his
  hands in the traverse direction and using holds, the leader
  attempts to move to the other side. In order to have, for a short
  time, both hands free it is advisable to abseil using a short
  Prusik sling as shown on p107. The most difficult traverses
  are those which are relatively long over steep, slippery rock
  and where there are only small differences in height. "The
  crossing by rope" is only possible with a well developed and
  trained sense of balance.
- Protection can be obtained by clipping the belay rope into the
  pitons inserted along the traverse. It is important to clip the
  belay rope under the traverse rope not over it.

The second follows along the fixed rope, both strands of which

a handrail rope

are fastened as tightly as possible by the leader to a safe piton using a clove hitch.

-   The second moves across keeping his hands on the fixed rope and takes out all the karabiners from the intermediate pitons.

The second can protect himself further by hanging from the fixed rope using a sling and karabiner (the sling should not be too short).

If the members of a roped party are climbing on twin ropes, they have to detach themselves from that one of the two ropes which is used as the traverse rope.

Please note! Rope traverses have to be climbed in the ascent direction only, not in the descent direction.

Pendulum traverse

A pendulum traverse is used to cross holdless vertical stretches of rock (a second rope is required). Under such circumstances, the use of a rope traverse is not possible. A pendulum traverse requires a piton placed as high as possible, the higher the piton the easier the

pendulum movement and, consequently, the longer the pendulum track. Here, just as in the case of a rope traverse, an accessory cord sling in the pendulum piton is necessary to recover the rope.

The pendulum movement is done using a figure of eight and a sit sling. In order to have both hands free for ease of movement it is recommended that the abseiling should be done with the protection of a Prusik sling as shown on p107. Belaying is done by putting the rope through the pendulum piton just as in the case of the rope traverse, or by a second piton. As this is a dynamic operation and the pendulum speed is considerable, the climbers must be absolutely sure that they have mastered the technique and that they possess good powers of response. Before using on longer traverses, this technique must be pracised in advance.

The pendulum manoeuvre uses the following procedure:

- The leader abseils from the pendulum piton across the section which is to be crossed. He begins the movement by pushing

sideways against the rock. With each pendulum swing the distance covered is increased.

- If at the maximum pendulum swing the leader is too high above his intended destination, then the procedure must be repeated to achieve a lower swing.
- The second follows in the same way and must recover the rope from the pendulum piton. The leader can help him by pulling on the belay rope.

Instead of abseiling with a figure of eight the climber can be lowered from the pendulum piton using an Italian hitch belay. This can save time as it is not necessary to sort out the rope. By this method the pendulum manoeuvre can be carried out using a single rope. This time the pendulum and belay ropes are the same. When the second has completed the pendulum then one of the two people must untie in order to recover the rope.

Please note! Just as with rope traverses, pendulum traverses, can be carried out in ascent only, not in descent.

THE USE OF THE ROPE WHEN SOLOING

Various methods of self belay can be chosen. All of them are quite complicated and the risk involved is always higher than when climbing as a member of a roped party because of the lack of a dynamic belay. This method effectively involves climbing routes three times - twice in ascent, once in descent.

Protection on short pitches
The distances between the running belays must be adjusted in relation to the length of the cow's tails (cow's tails plus radius of movement). The length of the cow's tails should be in accordance with the desired length (in most cases not longer than 2 - 3 metres). This means that the required rope length is as follows: twice the length of the cow's tail plus 3 metres for the 3 knots. Tie on approximately in the middle of the length of rope with a threaded double overhand knot (tied first as a single knot then thread the other end through) or with a threaded double figure of eight knot at each end.

After clipping one cow's tail into the first piton climb to the next one and clip in the other cow's tail. Then climb back down to the first piton and remove the cow's tail. Climb up to the second piton and then continue as before.

When climbing unbelayed both cow's tails have to be carried so as not to get in the way (carry as shoulder slings).

Protection on longer pitches

The distance between runners can be larger. Protection over the total rope length is possible. Tie on at the end of the rope. The other (loose) rope end is fixed in the anchor piton at the stance using a double figure of eight knot. During climbing the rope is clipped into every runner. A Prusik sling fastened to the harness (rope attachment loops) is at the same time attached to the rope in order to reduce the possible fall length (Prusik knot must have rope twisted 3 times round).

Beware! In the event of a fall the risks are higher than normally supposed. Various problems may occur. The following points have to be borne in mind:

- The Prusik sling may break under larger fall loads (melt due to heat). In this way fall length is increased.
- Because of this fact it is advisable to use a multi-fall rope and 6 mm dia accessory cord.

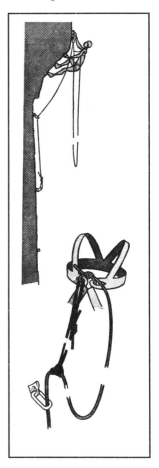

- It is only possible to foresee very small falls. Therefore sufficient numbers of runners have to be provided.
- The Prusik knot has to be checked in advance to ensure that it provides an adequate blocking effect.

To remove runners and karabiners, descend and climb back up as follows:

Climb down protected by a Prusik knot (or ascender) on the rope anchored above.

Climb back up either with protection from the Prusik knot (or with ascenders just as in the descent), or ascend with help of two Prusik slings (or with ascenders) using the conventional Prusiking technique.

THE USE OF THE ROPE FOR ABSEILING

At an abseiling place a safe fixing point is always required. It is possible to achieve loads of up to three times body weight.

Setting up the abseil point
The following may be used as natural fixing points for abseiling :
- rock spikes
- chockstones or threads

The strength should be checked first. A hammer should be used to remove any sharp rock edges. Use accessory cord slings of at least 6mm dia, tape slings of at least 20 mm width, otherwise any slings should be doubled before use. The tape slings should be joined by means of the tape knot. CAUTION - take care when abseiling slings are found! For safety reasons, older or damaged slings must be replaced.

In an emergency the rope can also be placed directly around a rock spike. However, the subsequent recovery is always considerably more difficult, or sometimes even impossible. In any case, it is harmful to the rope!

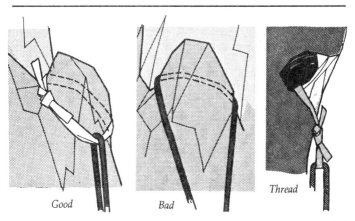

Good   *Bad*   *Thread*

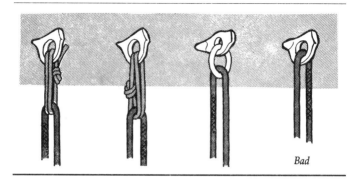

Bad

If there is no natural anchor available for fixing the abseil, it is necessary to make one. For this purpose the following may be used:

- rock pitons
- chocks

To be able to recover the rope more easily, after abseiling, the piton eye is "extended" with a short accessory cord sling or tape sling.

If a piton or chock is not sufficiently secure, a second one must be provided. They should be connected by an accessory cord sling or tape sling in such way as to load them as evenly as possible under

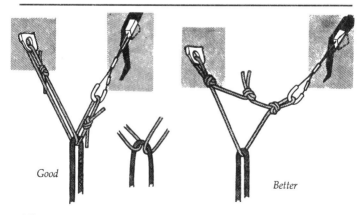

Good

Better

every likely angle of loading.

The rope will be passed through the anchor sling (in some cases through the piton ring). The rope should be pulled through in such way that its centre is placed at the anchor point. If double ropes are used, then the knot (reef knot, tape sling knot or double overhand knot) should be slightly below the anchor point. The rope ends are joined with a double overhand knot.

Afterwards the rope is picked up in arm-long loops. The last loops (those next to the anchor point) at the top, and they are thrown in a high curve away from the rock. If, in the course of this procedure, the rope becomes snagged, it must be pulled up and thrown down again.

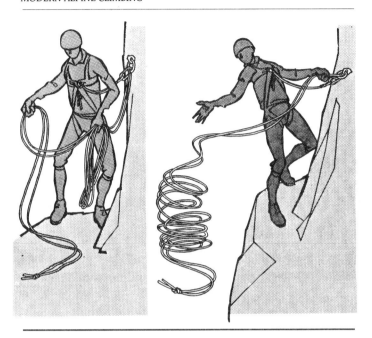

Abseiling with Figure of Eight

This is the most pleasant and simplest abseiling method. The necessary rope friction is produced in the figure of eight and by means of the braking hand (the hand below the figure of eight). This method is also still the best one in the event of wet ropes.

A bight of the abseiling rope is passed through the larger eye of the figure of eight and laid over the smaller one. One hand is used as leading hand, the other as braking hand. Only karabiners with a locking gate (e.g. screw gate karabiner) should be used, otherwise two karabiners should be hung with the spine of one against the gate of the other.

When bent figures of eight are used, different braking forces are necessary for double and single ropes.

After abseiling has been completed, the figures of eight should be removed from contact with the rope immediately, as they may be very hot (damaging the rope, nylon).

Abseil Procedure

Ready for abseiling, with hands on the rope, the climber descends until the abseil anchor point is at least level with his head, or somewhat higher. Only then does the abseiling start. During abseiling the legs should be stretched out in a flexible manner against the rock to prevent the unpleasant turning around the body axis. As to the function of hands, the following should be borne in mind:

- The leading hand is the hand on the tight rope (above the figure of eight). This hand is used to keep the upper part of the

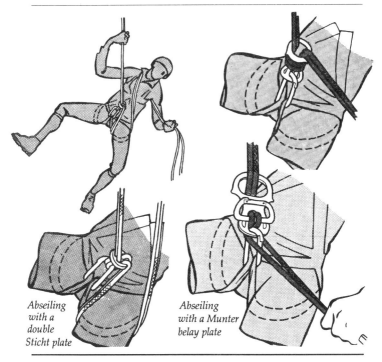

Abseiling with a double Sticht plate

Abseiling with a Munter belay plate

body in an upright position. Beginners often use it as a braking hand (this is wrong and is very strenuous).

- The hand on the loose rope (below the figure of eight) is the braking hand, controlling the speed of descent. Strong braking gives slow abseiling down to stopping; less strong braking gives faster abseiling.

With experience braking can be done with both hands on the free rope on the downside of the abseil device.

Beware - Abseiling should not be done too quickly. This can damage the rope through heat and the palms of the hands can get burned. WARNING - Any loose clothing, tape slings or long hair can become snagged in the figure of eight stopping the descent and

trapping the climber. Freeing the figure of eight can only be done by removing all load from it. Avoid any loose clothing etc when abseiling.

When descending steep or overhanging rock, the tight rope may lie directly on the rock and then the leading hand must be moved from above the contact point to hold the rope below.

If it is necessary to stop during abseiling and if both hands are needed for another activity (disentangling/unravelling the rope not hanging down loosely, etc.), then the loose rope is locked, by winding it around the thigh - as shown in the diagram.

Take care to ensure that the rope cannot fall down the leg.

After the first climber has abseiled, he frees himself from the rope (by disconnecting the abseil device). He then informs his partner above, by calling "Rope free", or "Rope O.K."

By monitoring the tension in the rope the partner above can tell as soon as the rope is free without further advice.

Abseiling with protection from above

A complicated way of protection. A second rope is obviously necessary. Advantage: the abseiling climber is always protected by means of a rope. The belay is carried out with an Italian hitch.

- The climber who is about to abseil is belayed by the other climber by means of the second rope. He may be anchored separately from the abseil anchor point. If the abseil anchor point is sufficiently reliable (which should be the rule), it is possible to use it for belaying as well. The belaying climber pays out the rope according to his partner's speed of descent.

- The next to abseil is belayed by the leader at the lower or bottom stance. In this case the rope runs from the lower to the upper stance and via the second anchor point (or the abseil anchor point) to the abseiling climber. The karabiner at the second piton may have to be left behind with this method (when using an accessory cord sling

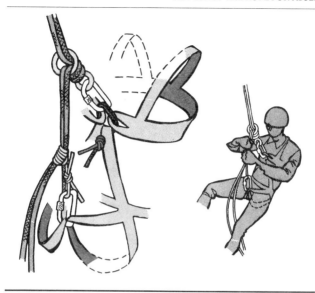

there is the danger of it breaking due to melting). Afterwards both ropes are recovered.

Abseiling with self-belay (self-securing).

The safest method, even for beginners. If the abseiling climber takes both his hands off the rope, the Prusik knot locks. The safest method for exhausted climbers as well. To continue abseiling, the Prusik knot is slid downwards with one hand.

- The figure of eight with the abseil rope inserted is clipped into the rope attachment loops of the harness (or into a sling threaded through them) using a screwgate karabiner (see diagrams). Below the figure of eight a short accessory cord sling with a Prusik knot is put around the rope and clipped into the sit part of the harness by means of a karabiner.
- The loose rope is held by both hands directly below the figure of eight and above the Prusik knot which is slid down the rope.

When stopping (to unravel the rope, etc.), the Prusik knot is removed.

Improvised sit sling

The karabiner seat is used, when the figure of eight is not available. The rope is used to produce the braking effect via the karabiner. Two different methods are possible: Rope twist and Italian hitch. Disadvantage is the tangling which can occur (especially with the Italian hitch).

- 3 rope twists (one rope twist = twisting through 180°, 3 rope twists = twisting through 3 x 180°)

- Italian hitch (used as in belaying but with the 2 ropes parallel).

WARNING - Put the rope over one shoulder otherwise the karabiner gate can open under load even if it has a safety lock. Handling is the

same as when using the figure of eight with the braking hand on the free rope, leading hand on the rope from above. Karabiners with locking devices (e.g. screwgate karabiners) should be used, otherwise two karabiners should be used so that the gate of one is opposite the spine of the other.

Recovery of the rope
Before the last person abseils , the party member who has just descended, checks if an easy recovery of the rope is possible (by pulling the rope). If the rope is jammed, the climber on the top must change the rope run at the anchor point and the possibility of a smooth rope recovery must be checked again.

When everyone has abseiled, the knot (at the bottom) is untied and the rope is recovered by pulling the easiest rope strand. With double ropes or twin rope, only the strand with the joining knot below the anchor point can be pulled.

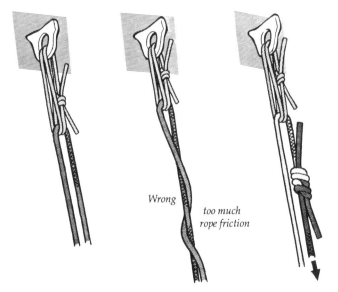

Wrong

too much rope friction

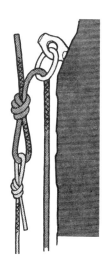

During recovery the rope should not be pulled too fast. This also applies to the moment, when the rope end slips through the abseil sling or through the piton ring. The danger of jamming the rope is greater when pulling quickly than with slow pulling. WARNING! Beware of stonefall! Stones may be dislodged by the falling rope.

ROCK CLIMBING FALLS AND
RESCUE TECHNIQUES

Any fall in the mountains, even a seemingly harmless one, may endanger life. It need not be a broken arm or leg, leaving out of consideration more serious injuries. Even a sprained ankle, the consequence of a harmless fall, may affect the progress of a roped party considerably, be it a necessary retreat or continued ascent. Any extension of a climbing tour on mountain terrain as far as time is concerned means an increase in the objective dangers (sudden change in weather, an unforeseen bivouac, etc.).

As a rule, in high mountains a roped party is alone. Many hours or even the whole day may pass before calls for help are heard and the mountain rescue is informed. Even then a rescue team must be put together and make arrangements on the spot. In the meantime, a sudden change in weather may lead even to the death of anyone who is injured (blood loss, shock effect, cold, hypothermia). The more remote the location in which an accident occurs, the longer it takes before a rescue team arrives. The same applies to higher grade climbs. Even if today helicopters are often used for rescue, their use still depends on good weather (visibility).

Therefore no deliberate risk of a fall should be taken in a mountain situation - there are enough risks of an unintentional fall. Approaching the margin of a fall should be reduced to a minimum and such risks should be taken only, when a reliable running belay is near at hand.

Nevertheless, if a fall cannot be avoided, then the climber should not simply fall "lifeless", but he should stretch all muscles (and sinews) and stop breathing to give the body more resisting power and elasticity thus trying to turn aside collisions with the rock. It is uncertain, however, if, in the event of a serious fall, such technique would bring the desired effect. There are too many unforeseen factors involved. Some good luck must also play a part. Falls on vertical rock are mostly not so dangerous as far as injuries are

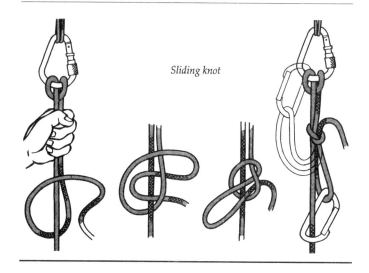

Sliding knot

concerned, provided there are running belays available and they can withstand the forces generated in the fall.

Securing the fallen climber.
After a fall, the climber who suffered the accident must be secured by the belayer who will need both hands free for first aid or rescue measures. For this purpose, a sliding knot is tied on the loose rope, behind the Italian hitch belay. This is then clipped into a karabiner at the anchor. Here, the advantage of the Italian hitch are obvious (this kind of belay would not at all be possible using the Sticht belay, and hardly possible with the karabiner cross belay and figure of eight belay). The sliding knot can be loosened by clipping out of the karabiner and pulling vigorously on the loose rope strand. Afterwards the fallen climber hangs protected by the Italian hitch again.

Prusiking up the fixed rope.
Two Prusik slings are required (ideally to be on hand ready for use at all times):

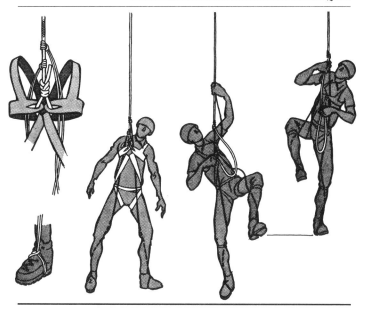

- diameter of the slings = 5mm (approximately half of the rope diameter);
- length of the slings = distance from foot up to the neck (not longer).

The slings are attached with the Prusik knot around the rope (when the ropes are wet or iced up one turn more should be applied), then passed between the chest harness and the chest then between the legs, around the outside of the leg and so to the foot (use slip knot over foot). Putting first one and then the other sling under load, both Prusik knots are alternately pushed upwards. The larger the single step, the faster the ascent. Other locking knots may also be used, just as may ascenders. The fastest and easiest to handle are those of the Jumar system.

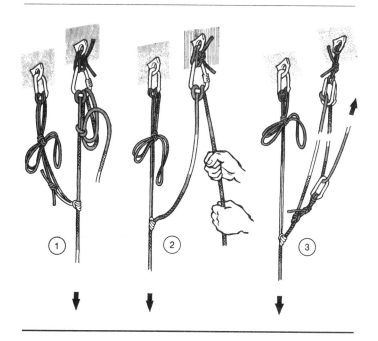

Pulley block technique

If the fallen climber is injured or unconscious, thus not being able to help himself, it is necessary to take rescue measures. As long as there is not too much friction of the rope on rock edges and in karabiners, a man can be pulled up by means of the AV (Alpenverein) single pulley block or the Swiss multiple pulley block. The procedure is as follows:

1. Secure the fallen climber by means of the sliding knot. A Prusik sling should be placed on the loaded rope and belayed by means of the Italian hitch and the sliding knot. This may also be done using the same piton (for clarity another piton has been shown in the diagram).

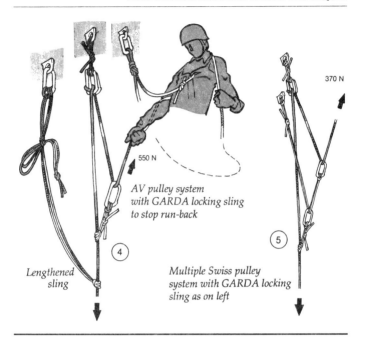

370 N

550 N

*AV pulley system
with GARDA locking sling
to stop run-back*

(4)

*Lengthened
sling*

(5)

*Multiple Swiss pulley
system with GARDA locking
sling as on left*

2. Loosen the sliding knot on the loaded rope, to let the load off and to transfer it to the Prusik sling.

3. Build up the AV pulley system with the Garda clamping sling.

4. To lift up by means of the pulley system until the Prusik sling is free from load (the sliding knot on the accessory cord serves only in emergencies, provided that the lifting movement is not sufficient to free the accessory cord from the load). The Prusik sling is then removed and the fallen climber has to be brought to safety.

5. If the pulling strength of the rescuer is insufficient, an accessory cord may be used to change the simple AV pulley system into the multiple Swiss pulley system.

RETREAT ON ROCK

With climbs up to grade II climbers usually descend the same route. By this method, the person descending first (the weaker member) can use - to save time - the rope as an occasional aid. This can go to such an extent that this person may be lowered, metre by metre, by the belayer using an Italian hitch belay.

Starting with grade III, descent by abseiling is used as a rule, provided it is not prevented by roofs and overhanging rocks. With 2 'double' ropes the retreat is far less complicated than with one

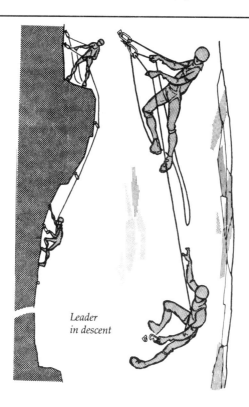

*Leader
in descent*

single rope (with the former case, abseiling can occur over a greater distance, while in the latter case, the abseil length may be as little as 20 metres). If not sure, set up a self-belay on the abseil rope. As far as it is possible, stay on the familiar route. Thus the existing anchor pitons on the stances can be used as abseiling pitons. Abseiling on difficult or unknown terrain should be attempted only when there is the prospect of finding a suitable stance within the abseiling length.

On overhanging rocks, a special retreat technique is required. With single rope, this can be carried out only over the half rope length. The procedure is as follows:

Second in descent

- The leader is lowered to about half the rope length by the second using an Italian hitch belay. In the course of descending he places all strategically important runners (ie. change of direction). He takes in the remaining rope at the stance.
- The second follows belayed by the leader from below with an Italian hitch belay but with the rope running through a karabiner at the previous (ie. upper) stance where a karabiner has to be sacrificed. (Warning! Do not use accessory cord as it breaks due to melting.)

   In order to be able to reach all the runners during his descent, the second clips a karabiner into his harness and onto the part of the rope between the upper stance and his belayer. While descending, the second removes all the runners.
- When at last reaching the lower stance, one of the two climbers unties (pay attention to any self belay when untied!) and the rope is recovered.

USE OF THE ROPE ON GLACIERS

On parts of a glacier free of snow (a dry glacier) all crevasses are clearly visible and can usually be by-passed safely. On glaciers covered with snow, crevasses are concealed which makes the glacier far more dangerous. An inexperienced climber may be misled by the (seemingly) harmless appearance of many glaciers covered with snow and behave carelessly.

As a matter of principle mountaineers must rope up on glaciers covered with snow. The rope is used for security and rescue in the event of a fall into a crevasse.

Roping up of itself, however, does not guarantee safety, and this also applies on glaciers. Only when correct safety techniques are applied can the roped party not only avoid the risk of a fall into a crevasse, but also have the ability to rescue a climber who has fallen into a crevasse.

Moving together when roped presents, on steep glacier slopes, the danger of being dragged along. If one member of the roped party falls, the other or others are dragged with him. The rope ensures the transfer of the force from one person to the other.

The same danger occurs on steep snowy slopes, when climbers ascend or descend simultanously when roped. One or more climbers on the same rope may be dragged together with their falling partner until the whole party arrives on less steep ground. If there is no possibility to belay by rope length from stance to stance on snow covered flanks due to lack of time or because the ground is not steep, then movement without rope - as long as there is no danger of crevasses - offers, after all, greater safety to the whole party than the movement roped. When the ice climber goes as an individual and falls, then after a short distance, he is able to stop his fall by using the life-saving ice axe braking technique, thus bringing the fall to a halt. On the other hand, partners of a rope team always drag each other into the depths (as claimed by members of roped parties who fell and survived).

This emphasises the importance of mastering the ice axe braking technique.

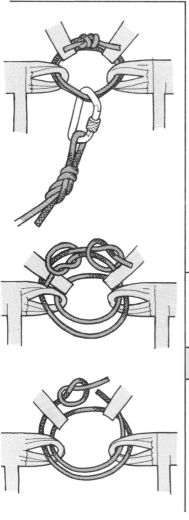

Roping up on glaciers

The roping up is done out with a separate accessory cord or tape sling attached to the harness into which a karabiner with a locking gate is clipped to enable the climber to detach himself from the main rope quickly and at any time, whenever a crevasse rescue appears to be necessary.

Accessory cord should be at least 6 mm diameter and 1.5m long. Tape must be at least 20mm wide (3 marking threads) and 1.5m long.

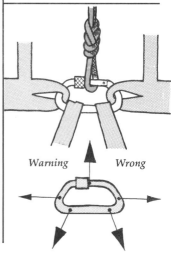

Warning   *Wrong*

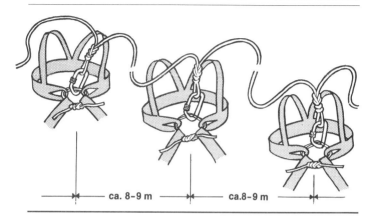

ca. 8–9 m   ca.8–9 m

WARNING! Never clip karabiners directly into the loops of a harness! This can lead to transverse forces and the karabiner could break.

How the climber is attached (ie. on which part of the rope), depends on the number of members of the roped party (two, three or four). (see the illustration) For tying on the double overhand knot or the double figure or eight knot is used.

Tying on with an accessory cord loop and a karabiner presents the danger of facial injuries, with a fall into a crevasse (the karabiner is snatched upwards). Nevertheless, this method has prevailed, as it is the most convenient technique in use.

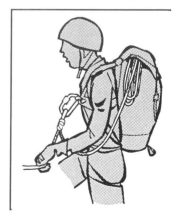

The slack rope between the climbers is taken up in arm-long loops and stowed under the rucksack flap (or, if there is no rucksack, carried over the shoulder). In this way, ropes are quickly available, if needed for crevasse rescue.

Moving on glaciers

As there is always the danger of crevasses, when traversing snow covered glaciers it is done as a roped team. In order to rescue a member of the roped party who falls into a crevasse as quickly as possible, the team members rope up at different places on the rope. This depends upon the number of team members (two, three or four).

In general, the most experienced member of the roped party, who has also the greatest stamina goes ahead (being able to make the route, probe the ground and search for glacier crevasses). The whole team move together and at the same speed. If possible, the rope should not trail along on the glacier. Rope loops are not coiled up and are not held in the hand. Exceptions: when openings might suddenly appear. Beware of hard snow crust. Beware of hidden crevasses.

The danger of crevasses on glaciers is very frequently underestimated. To recognise such dangers is made more difficult with

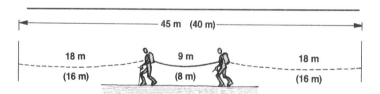

On steep ground (risk of falling into crevasses) two man rope team with somewhat larger distance about 10m to 12m

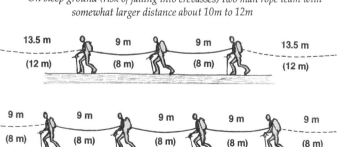

newly-fallen snow and haze (diffused light reduces shadows). Carelessness and lack of experience may also bring about a fall into a crevasse.

Glacier crevasses should always be crossed at right angles with their line, the wider ones can be crossed by jumping over with a few steps approach (not more than three or four steps). Warning! There must be enough rope available to allow jumping. Rope loops should be taken up and dropped as appropriate when jumping. The

Leader checking for crevasse

Beware crevasse in deeply sunken areas

opposite side of a crevasse must be safe enough to support landing after the jump (it should always be checked).

Even wider crevasses must be by-passed at a safe distance (the snow cornice in crevasses cannot be checked).

Before crossing a snow bridge, the leader has to check, with the ice axe, its ability to support a load. All other members of the roped party wait in safety as far as possible from the edge of the crevasse. If necessary the second team member unties and, shortly before the third reaches the spot, ties on the rope again (this provides a counterpoise for the possible fall of the leader into a crevasse). If probing with the axe finds a hollow, retreat immediately. The bridge is thin and it is unlikely to be capable of carrying load.

If crevasse bridges are to be crossed which do not seem safe enough (and bypassing the crevasse is not possible), then it is necesary to crawl. The ice axe has to be held in both hands to keep the surface load as low as possible.

Long, narrow cracks always indicate crevasses. There are always less crevasses in glacier valleys (concave) than on glacier ridges (convex).

CREVASSE FALL AND RESCUE TECHNIQUES

A force of between 200N and 500 N (approximately from 20 kgf to 50 kgf), whether horizontal or diagonal, is likely to pull someone over. A member of a roped party falling into a crevasse cannot therefore be held by the second, whether moving or standing. The sudden force will cause him to fall to the ground and be dragged along in the direction of the crevasse edge until the fall energy is used up by the friction of the rope at the crevasse edge and by friction between the falling climber and the surface of the glacier (in

Crevasse fall on a steep glacier. The force of the fall by this method is very dangerous for the remaining rope members. Rope friction on the crevasse edge and between the falling climber and the surface of the glacier is often insufficient to hold the fall. The remaining rope members then follow the leader into the crevasse.

the form of friction work). Only then has the crevasse fall been held. Occasionally, those dragged to the ground receive arm dislocations and/or bone fractures.

In the case of a three-member roped party the third one is also usually pulled to the ground. The braking length in the direction of the crevasse edge is then shorter. Here and in the description of crevasse rescue which follows, the advantages of three and four-member roped parties are clearly demonstrated. The two-member team comes off worst.

To prevent the risk of being dragged along with the others, a series of short 'double overhand knots on the bight' can be tied on the rope, by means of which the friction on the crevasse edge is considerably increased, but the crevasse rescue is not impeded.

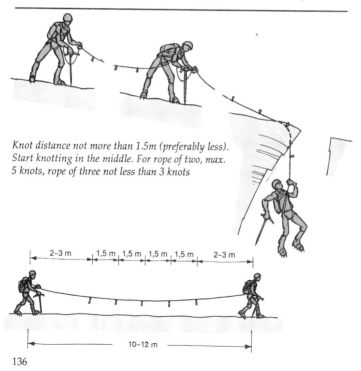

Knot distance not more than 1.5m (preferably less). Start knotting in the middle. For rope of two, max. 5 knots, rope of three not less than 3 knots

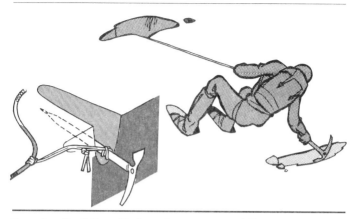

Securing the fallen climber after a crevasse fall

After the crevasse fall has been stopped, the fallen climber must be secured. The more roped partners who are available, the better. If the rope party consists of two people only, then the one dragged to the ground must do the securing in an unfavourable position.

First of all, an anchor must be created. Only the buried ice axe is likely to be useful. It offers the safest anchorage on hard snow (an ice-axe rammed in vertically is not at all reliable). With experience, the buried ice axe anchor can be fixed quite easily within a few minutes. For the actual buried anchor the following may be used:

- technical ice axe, normal ice axe, ice hammer;
- rucksack (an empty one is best);
- (articles of) clothing (anorak, pullover,large gloves).

The procedure of fixing is as follows:

- To cut a groove in the snow, at right angles to the direction of the loaded rope, using the ice axe or ice hammer (in emergency with hands, gloves). The groove should be as narrow as possible but sufficiently deep. The smaller the anchor (ice hammer, gloves), the deeper the groove (at least 50 cm).
- To make a narrow groove (for the accessory cord), at right angles to the main groove and in the direction of the loaded rope.
- To put a sling around the loaded rope and to fasten it to the anchor with a Prusik knot.
- To push the anchor as deeply as possible into the groove (the pick of an ice tool pointing downwards). To pile up and to stamp down the snow over the anchor (take snow from the side which is not to be loaded!).
- To carefully slacken the loaded rope and to transfer the load slowly to the Prusik sling and the anchor.
- To get out of the rope (to open the karabiner and to loosen the rope knot).

If there are other members of the roped party available, the person who carries out the anchoring is supported by them by pulling the rope using the weight of their own bodies. The other people may even do the anchoring themselves. Afterwards they untie from the rope so that the rescue from the crevasse can begin (using a roller or a pulley block). Beware of other crevasses! Self anchor with a Prusik sling should be made at the anchor point or using the unloaded rope!

It is not possible to rescue a partner of approximately the same weight with bare hands, or without using an ancillary tool. The rope cuts into the crevasse edge (causing friction!). Thus the required pulling force is increased considerably. Various methods of crevasse rescue are on offer. The choice depends on the number of rescuers available, and the methods are dealt with below.

Team haul

The simplest and fastest type of crevasse rescue which requires, however, a sufficient number of the roped partners and/or helpers (possibly another roped party which may be near). A person hanging freely in the crevasse can be rescued by the simultaneous pulling of four men (five or more would be even better). (The pulling force of one man is approximately 400 N, ie. approx 40 kgf.) While doing this, precise commands have to be given and obeyed. The procedure is as follows:

- Following the command "Hold - Pull" (with emphasis on "Pull"), the rescuers pull simultaneous. The pull takes place above a Prusik knot attached to the anchor point.
- After each lift the three rescuers (or more, as the case may be) hold the rope firmly for a short time, while the one nearest the anchor point slides the Prusik knot as far as possible in the direction of the crevasse edge.
- A short rest follows.
- The rope is grasped again and, following a command, the next lifting movement begins.

Short double overhand knots on the pulling rope make the grasping and pulling easier.

Climbing over the crevasse edge is always difficult for the person being rescued. Helping hands at the crevasse edge are not useful. It is better to arrange a rope or an accessory cord sling fastened to the anchor point and which can be used as a hold. If this, combined with front point technique, is still not enough, the sling has to be extended in order to be used as a foot loop.

If the crevasse edge is overhanging, then the person to be rescued has to make a breach in it. This can also be done by the rescuers, but not, when the head of the person in the crevasse is just below! Caution in any case! If the ice axe pick is used, there is a danger of damaging the rope.

When the person being rescued is just below an overhanging

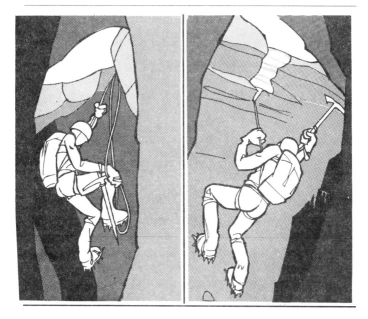

edge, care must be applied when pulling the rope to avoid injuring him.

Roller

The fastest and least complicated rescue method suitable for roped parties of any size. The pulley principle is utilised. For this purpose a certain amount of free rope is required, the length of which is at least twice the distance between the anchor point and the climber hanging in the crevasse (assuming that there is enough rope available).

After the climber who has fallen into the crevasse has been secured, the procedure is as follows:

- A rope loop with a karabiner attached is dropped down to the climber hanging in the crevasse.
- The climber clips the karabiner into his harness tie-on point.

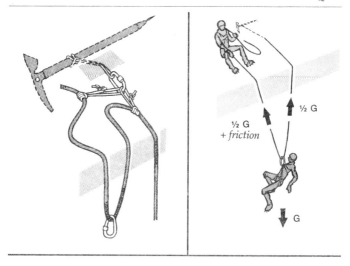

- Following a command the rescuer - or rescuers - pull on the rope. After each lifting movement the rope is held tightly for a short time while the Prusik knot is pushed along the rope in the direction of the crevasse edge. Afterwards the next lifting movement follows.
- The climber to be rescued can assist this work substantially by pulling himself upwards on the fixed rope during each lifting movement (on the rescuers' command) in this way the rope friction is decreased.

Exiting from the crevasse is as in the event of the straight team pull. All other rescue methods require more time. Pulleys (pages 62 and 142) decrease friction so that the work of lifting is made easier.

Pulley

A method suitable for a roped party of two, when the second climber is not strong enough to use the roller method. In this case the roller is mounted in a single pulley block and is used as follows:

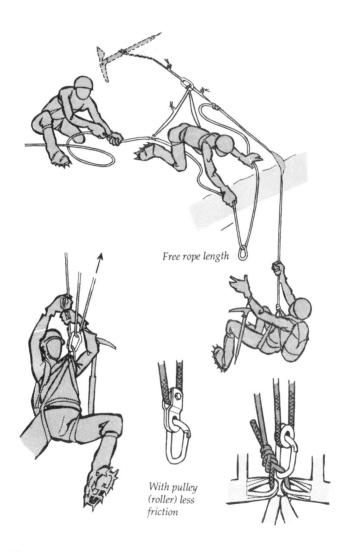

Free rope length

With pulley
(roller) less
friction

Garda locking sling to stop running back

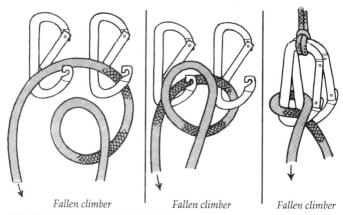

Fallen climber	*Fallen climber*	*Fallen climber*

- The rope loop, with the karabiner clipped in, is lowered (as with the roller method) to the climber hanging in the crevasse. He then clips the karabiner into his harness tie on point.
- The free rope end is threaded through the pulley: a Garda sling for holding temporarily and short Prusik sling with a karabiner are attached to the rope coming from the pulley.
- Every lifting movement should be carried out with the karabiner close to the Garda fixing sling. Afterwards the Prusik knot is again slid down the rope as far as possible in the direction of the crevasse edge.
- The next lifting movement follows.

The larger the distance between the Garda fixing sling and the crevasse edge, the better (the working strokes can be larger) so that the climber hanging in the crevasse can be rescued more quickly.

Exiting over the crevasse edge is done as in the case of pulling by the team members.

Combining a roller and a single pulley block is the principle of the double pulley block. Hence also double the work is done and the job completed in half the time.

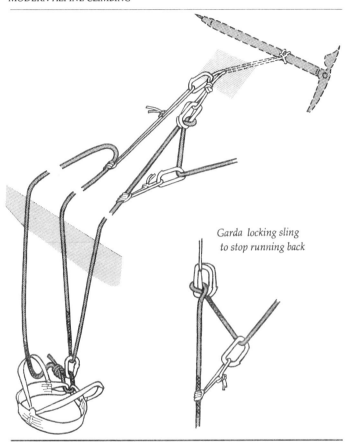

*Garda locking sling
to stop running back*

Prusik technique

A method applicable when the "rescuer(s)" is (are) too weak or do not know what to do, but the climber who has fallen into the crevasse is still capable of action and has two Prusik slings on hand (it should be the rule to have Prusik slings already attached to the rope and to stow them in a trouser pocket).

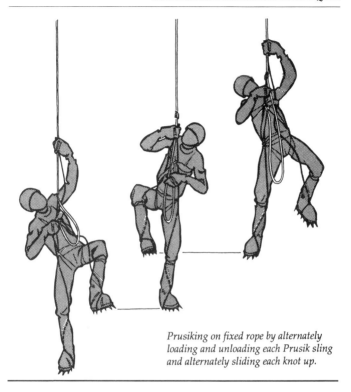

Prusiking on fixed rope by alternately loading and unloading each Prusik sling and alternately sliding each knot up.

The procedure is the same as in the case of prusiking on rock (see p.122).

When exiting over the crevasse edge, the unloaded Prusik knot must be removed. The best way is to get a second rope loop passed down from above and to tie into it the second Prusik knot, or to step in a lowered accessory cord sling.

USE OF THE ROPE ON STEEP ICE

A fall on steep ice is hardly less severe than one on rock. The fall on a 60° steep snow or ice slope corresponds to about a 90% free fall. Because fewer runners are used as a general rule on snow and ice, the falls are mostly longer. Safe and sound techniques with the ice axes(s), crampons and anchoring are therefore of special importance.

On steep ice the rope is used - just as on rock - for protection, and is handled in the same way. Only one climber of the roped party moves at once, being belayed by the other at the stance (ice screw, ice piton). For the handling of the rope, the same commands apply as on rock.

Simultaneous movement when roped is - just as on rock - not advisable. In the event of a fall of one roped partner, the second or the others are also carried along.

If there is a three member roped party (one leader climbing ahead, two followers climbing behind on separate ropes), then the leader is belayed by only one of the two followers (should both belay, each of them at one rope, the force in the event of a fall would double). Both followers are belayed by the leader simultaneously on both ropes.

Movement of two-man rope team

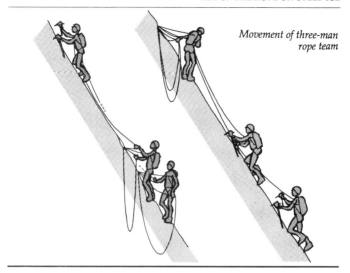

Movement of three-man rope team

The climbers tie onto the end of the rope (just as on rock). When belaying, an allowance for a sufficient braking reserve should be made. A 40m pitch therefore requires at least 45m of rope.

Belay to the anchor by means of the Italian hitch (two ice screws or one ice screw/one ice piton, using a force triangle).

The stance may have to be cut out by the ice axe. Wear a helmet! Pieces of ice falling from a height of 40m have an enormous impact energy.

As the ground gets steeper, towards the boundary of safe movement, runners must be placed often, the first one at after not more than half the rope length (typically at 20m distance). The steeper the ice slope the shorter the intervals.

Belaying on snow and ice slopes

The Italian hitch is handled just as on rock. Two fixing points are advisable at the stance. There should be a distance of about ¹/₂ metre between the two ice screws, or between the ice screw and the ice piton (do not use two ice pitons). Connect the two by means of a

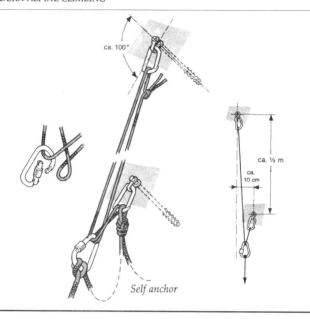

ca. 100°

ca. ½ m

ca. 10 cm

Self anchor

force triangle (leading) to a central belay point (just as on rock). Self-anchor at one of the two anchor points.

Belaying of the leader and of the following climber(s) is the same as on rock. This also applies to the stance change, where there is only one leader.

If the belayed climbers falls, the fall should be braked by an instinctive closing of the braking hand.

When anchoring with a buried axe, in principle, the same procedure is used as when belaying at ice screws and ice pitons. A double overhand knot or a double figure of eight knot is tied into the anchor sling, into which the Italian hitch karabiner is clipped. The self-anchor to the anchor is clipped in above the knot.

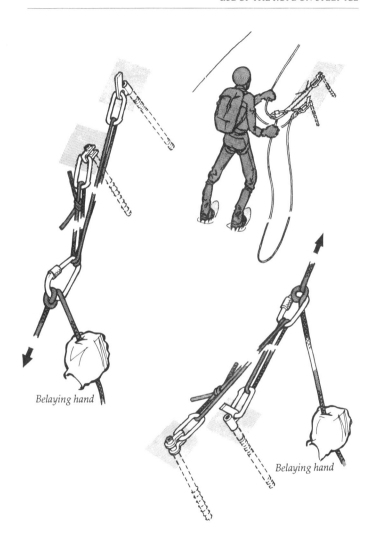

Belaying hand

Belaying hand

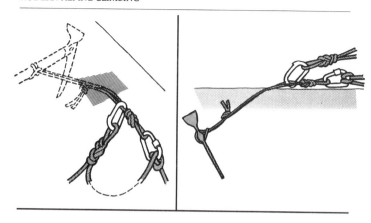

Belaying using the buried axe method is carried on in a similar way.
A double overhand or figure of eight knot is tied in the accessory cord and the
HMS karabiner is clipped in. The self anchor is made above the knots

BELAYING ON SNOW AND ICE RIDGES

There may be great differences in the form of snow and ice ridges. A distinction must be drawn between the following formations:

- broad snow and ice ridges with or without the danger of a (snow) cornice,
- narrow snow and ice ridges, steeply sloping on both sides, with or without the danger of (snow) cornice.

The movement, protection and behaviour of the team, in the event of a fall of one of its members, must be adjusted to the form of the ridge, as described on the following pages.

The members of the team are roped on as on the glacier (with an accessory cord sling tied into the harness tie-on loops, into which a locking gate karabiner is clipped), the distance between each person being approximately 8 to 9m. This is the fastest way to prepare for different situations. If the form of the ridge changes, the response must be adjusted to the new situation.

It is not always possible to determine the shape of the ridge on both sides. If the ridge turns flatter, there is always the danger of cornices on the sheltered side. The ground should be probed with the ice axe. Sufficient distance should be kept from the possible breaking-off line (see p.153), so that the point probed with the ice axe is not nearer than approximately one metre from that line. The cornice can be so thick that the ice axe cannot penetrate to the underside.

Every ridge which becomes flatter could tempt the climbers to move on its crest. Sufficient distance must always be kept from the suspect breaking-off line, even if the climbers are forced to take a less pleasant line on a steeper slope.

In the event of a fall of one member of the roped party on a narrow snow or ice ridge, the next one on the rope must jump down the opposite side of the ridge. Initially, everybody dislikes such a jump, as it does not correspond with the natural reaction. It must therefore be practised in advance! Begin on less steep snow ridges which slope down only a few metres. Without such practice, prospects for success decrease rapidly, as even a few second of hesitation may cause the second to be dragged after the leader.

Protection with the rope on snow ridges may be dispensed with only under specific conditions without the danger of cornices breaking off (see in this respect p.153).

Broad snow and ice ridges without danger of the cornice breaking off
The least dangerous type of ridge, usually horizontal. (Ridges on the shoulder or crest of mountains.)

The roped climbers move together. The distance from one person to the next ranges approximately from 8 to 9 metres (as on the glacier).

If the course of the ridge becomes steeper, the movement is similar to that on sloping snow and ice flanks (because of the danger of being dragged away).

Depending on the steepness and on the capability of the roped team, the simultaneous movement may continue, or it

Wide snow and ice ridge without risk of breaking cornice

may be necessary to belay from stance to stance as well as to carry out self-anchoring.

Broad snow and ice ridges with the danger of the cornices breaking off
The roped party moves together keeping sufficient distance from the possible break-off line. The distance between each person should be approximately from 8 to 9 metres (as on the glacier). Each of them holds in his hand several loose rope coils in order to be able to jump immediately to the other side of the ridge, should the cornice break-off.

When the above-mentioned distance from one roped team mem-

Wide snow and ice ridges with risk of breaking cornice

ber to the other is maintained, then during a fall due to the cornice breaking off, the rope cutting into the snow, together with the remaining roped party members acting as a counterweight, provides sufficient braking.

Due to the levelling off of the ridge, the climbers may be enticed into a more relaxed movement on the top of the ridge. However, it is important to maintain a sufficient safety distance from the possible break-off line.

Narrow snow and ice ridges sloping on both sides, without the danger of the cornice breaking off
Simultaneous movement on the rope. Distance between each person, approximately 8 and 9 metres (just as on the glacier). Each

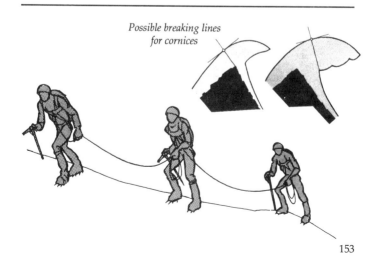

Possible breaking lines for cornices

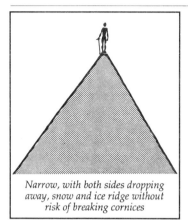

Narrow, with both sides dropping away, snow and ice ridge without risk of breaking cornices

member of the roped team holds a few loose rope coils in his hand in order to be able to jump immediately to the opposite side of the ridge, should a team member fall.

The counterweight effect from jumping over the other side and the cutting of the rope into the snow brings the fall to a standstill. This can also protect the third and/or fourth members of a roped party providing the distances are maintained and loops are dropped so as to avoid anyone being dragged after the falling climber.

It is advisable to let the weaker climber move ahead in order to keep an eye on him. If the team members are equal as to capability and experience and if there is no cornice, the rope may be dispensed with.

Sharp, with both sides falling steeply, snow and ice ridge with risk of breaking cornice

Sharp snow and ice ridges, sloping steeply on both sides, with the danger of the cornice breaking off

A line must be taken below the crest of the ridge (below the possible break-off line) on the steep ground, even if this becomes more and more difficult and time consuming.

As a rule, there is no simultaneous movement anymore, but belayed movement from stance to stance (belaying the mem-

bers of the roped team as well as anchoring oneself). The distance between the stances may be chosen less than 40 metres. Runners are recommended, according to steepness.

If the ground below the ridge is less steep and there is not much time - the climbers move simultaneously. There is, however, the danger of being dragged along, should a team member fall. Movement without the rope is therefore advisable (just as on sloping snow and ice flanks).

RETREAT ON ICE

As far as possible, the ascent track should be followed when descending. Thus the previously cut stances in ice walls can be used again. The climber descending first is belayed (down) by his partner using an Italian hitch. Thus he can descend fast and safely, as less attention is required. In the event of steeper and more difficult passages (eg. a blank ice wall) runners must be fixed for the second climber following from above. During the descent the full rope length should not be paid out, but sufficient braking reserve for belaying should be saved!

If it is necessary to abseil and if there are not sufficient ice screws and/or ice pitons, an "ice pear" (bollard) can be cut out (very time-consuming). This bollard must not be too small (the smallest diameter at least the length of the forearm), the larger it is, the higher the load-bearing capacity.

A self extracting abseil anchor with an ice screw is difficult to

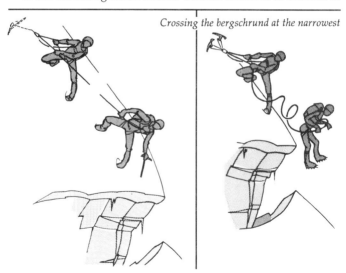

Crossing the bergschrund at the narrowest

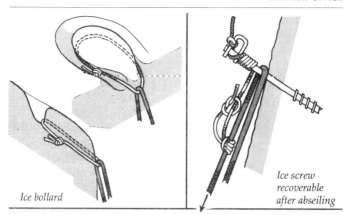

Ice bollard

Ice screw recoverable after abseiling

achieve. If the ice screw is set in deep, it is not possible to loosen it after abseiling. If the screw is less deep, it can break out during abseiling. In any case, it should be carefully checked first.

Crossing the bergschrund should be done at the narrowest and lowest place, as shown in the diagrams.

and lowest place as shown in these four pictures

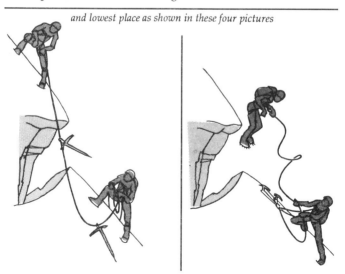

FIXED ROPES ON ICE

On expeditions above the snow line in mountain regions outside Europe, fixed ropes are frequently used for repeated ascents and descent. Fixing of these ropes as well as movement and belay by means of them is different from the techniques covered so far.

Because of weight (air freight) thin half ropes are used (twin ropes). The security of the anchor point must be preserved for a longer period of time. Snow stakes and ice screws can soften under the effect of solar radiation, and, besides, their transportation is very expensive (air freight). Better alternatives are available.

"T" anchoring with wood

The best and safest fixing point. During the walk in, some pieces of wood are collected in the last wooded stretch (newly felled wood or branches, no rotten wood).

Dimensions: length from 70 to 90cm, thickness from 4 to 5cm - (wrist diameter). They have to be dug into the snow sufficiently deep (not less than 50cm)!

Vertically rammed-in wood

Thicker branches can also be rammed in. Short side branches, or stumps of such branches can prevent the accessory cord sliding up whilst ramming the wood in.

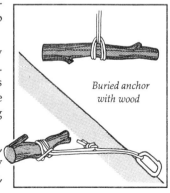

Buried anchor with wood

- Diameter of the accessory cord should be at least 5mm.
- Fresh wood logs as anchors hold even better, if they are wetted first (eg. by urinating on them!).

When snow stakes are used, they must be rammed in deeply enough and covered with snow,

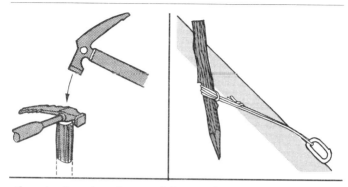

otherwise there is an increased danger of melting.

The fixed ropes are fastened to the accessory cord slings of the anchor points using double overhand or double figure of eight knots. Fixed ropes must not be set tight (danger of melting through) - the ropes should hang loosely.

Threaded anchors on ice
Anchor points on solid ice can be made by "tunnelling" into the ice (the "Abalakov" method). If the holes are sufficiently deep (at least 15cm), then the breaking force, measured vertical to the hole axes,

Thread in ice

90°   90°

ranges from 6 to 8 kN (ca 600 to 800 kgf). There is no danger of melting. The holes in the ice (tunnelling) are drilled with a tubular ice screw. The accessory cord can more easily be passed through with the help of a short piece of wire with a pointed hook.

Ascent and descent on fixed ropes

Tie on just as when traversing glaciers, with chest and sit harnesses joined by means of an accessory cord loop. Chest and sit harness can be connected with the figure of eight (see page 69). Movement and belaying on the fixed rope is done by means of an ascender using the Jumar principle. The Petzl model is best, as clipping in and out of the fixed rope can comfortably be done with one hand only (also with gloves on). The ascender is clipped into the sit harness by means of an arm-long accessory cord.

When moving upwards the ascender is pushed up at the same time. Under a sudden downwards load it locks (such as a pull, in

case of a fall or a sudden stop).

Ascent and descent are done in three stages:

- to push the ascender upwards and hold it firmly
- to step up with one foot and to straighten the leg
- to step up with the other foot.

When stationary, the climber hangs from the ascender via the sit harness. Balance with legs slightly apart. The upper part of the body is support by the accessory cord.

In descent the ascender's operating lever must be held loose but not so that the clamp cannot work.

Each ascender in turn must be uncoupled and reconnected at the anchor points. The weight is on the legs slightly apart and with one hand on the rope. The clamp is released and the ascender is then removed from the rope and when the anchor point has been passed, it is clipped in again. The rope is secured by the clamp again (partly automatic because of spring mechanism). The ascent then continues.

In the event of very steep ascents, two ascenders are advisable. Vertical ascent of the fixed rope with two ascenders only and with a foot loop on each rope fastened with a Prusik knot.

THE ALPINE DISTRESS SIGNAL

The alpine distress signal is used in emergencies only. The signal can be visual or acoustic (shouting, whistling, flash light signal, opening and closing a bivi bag or bright clothing which may be visible over the widest possible distance). The distress signal is performed as follows:

- chosen signal at regular intervals, six times within one minute, ie. intervals of 12 seconds between each one.
- this is followed by a one minute break, whereupon the signal is repeated.

The distress signal is continued until a reply is received. Even then the signal must not be stopped fully. Repetition over longer periods (of time) is important to guide the rescuers to the team's position, and also to let them know that their help is still required.

The rescuers response is as follows:

- one signal at regular intervals, three times within one minute, ie. intervals of 30 seconds between each one.
- this is followed by a one minute break, whereupon the signal is repeated.

The alpine distress signal is printed on the reverse side of Alpine Club membership cards.

In countries such as France, Italy and the Western Alps regions,

a distress signal is used which is visible far away. A square red cloth (1m x 1m) with a white ring (inner diameter 60cm, width of the ring 15cm) is displayed in such a way that it can be recognised from the direction from which help is expected.

During recent years it has become necessary to develop new methods of communication as the use of helicopters for rescue purposes in emergencies in the mountains has been on the increase. For visual communication arm signals and colour light signals of the following kind have been established:

Signal		Meaning
To hold both arms diagonally upwards		"Yes" reply to questions asked
Light signal of any colour		Land here We need help
To hold the left arm diagonally upwards and the right arm diagonally downwards No light signals		"No" reply to questions asked Do not land No help required

The signals with the arms are derived from 'Y' in the word YES, and from 'N' in NO. Please note! As mentioned above, each light signal means that help is required. There are no rules about the possible meaning of "red" = help, "green" = no help.

Smoke signals, marks in the snow and the brightness of anorak colours make it easier to find the climbers in danger from the air.

When an accident is reported to the mountain rescue service, the information must be brief and precise. Try to remember the 5 W's (5 W scheme):

- WHAT has happened (nature of the accident, number of injured)
- WHEN did the accident happen?
- WHERE did the accident happen, where is the injured person (refer to map or guidebook)
- WHO has been injured, who is reporting the accident (personal data)
- WEATHER in the area, where the accident happened (eg. visibility).

It is impossible for the helicopter pilot to land in many locations or to take the injured. There are the following points which must therefore be considered:

1. A flat or horizontal place of ca 20m x 20m, not involving a banking turn and not in a narrow ravine.

2. Secure equipment against the wind caused by the rotor. This could be dangerous for the helicopter!

3. Obstacles within 100m of the taking off and landing area should not he higher than 15m! beware of cable-car wires and electricity cables!

4. Stamp down firmly any soft powdery snow over an area of 20m x 20m!

5. Indicate wind direction! Stand with the back against the wind, arms sidewards, stay in front of the landing place until the helicopter rotor stops!

6. Wait until the rotor stops or until the pilot indicates that the helicopter can be approached!

7. Approach the helicopter only from the front or below and bend down when near it!

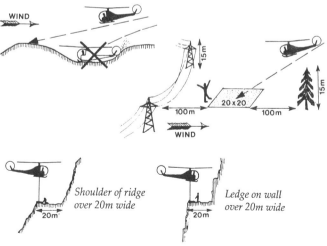

Shoulder of ridge over 20m wide

Ledge on wall over 20m wide

A LITTLE BELAYING THEORY

Belaying theory encompasses the processes which take place in the rope during a fall and when the rope is under the load as well as the "responses" of the rope to other components of the safety chain such as pitons, karabiners, chocks, adjustable chocks, slings and harnesses (chest and sit).

Which belaying system - static or dynamic?
Two belaying systems are possible, each with a different effect:

- Static belaying methods jam the rope under load in the event of a fall, which means that there is no rope run-through.
- Dynamic belaying methods allow - when the rope is under load in the case of a fall - a controlled rope run-through, as a suitable braking device is provided (operated by another member of the roped team) which continues until the fall is stopped.

Static belaying methods develop the maximum forces in all the components of the safety chain which in the event of a fall with a significant fall factor result in a high impact force in the rope. The reliability of the anchor points is usually assessed for normal loadings and with such higher forces this reliability is placed in question.

Dynamic belaying methods reduce the high impact force and the forces in the safety chain are considerably diminished (see diagram on the page 166). The useful range of belaying forces lies between 2 and 4 kN (between 200 and 400 kgf).

The rope run-through in the braking device (operated by another team member) is compensated by extension of the rope under load at the time of maximum impact so that the fall length is kept within manageable limits, when compared with static belaying methods. Runners also reduce the rope run-through by friction in the karabiner so that, as a rule, the fall length is reduced even further.

To optimise the chances of the survival of the whole roped team,

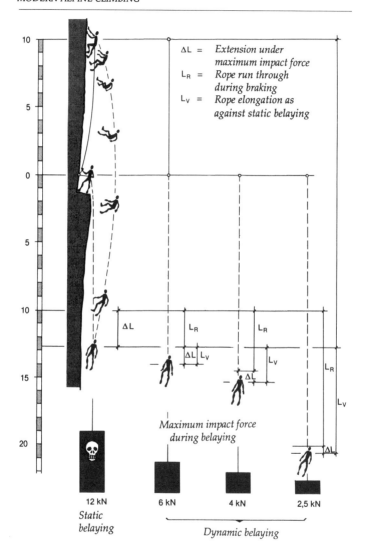

ΔL = Extension under maximum impact force

L$_R$ = Rope run through during braking

L$_V$ = Rope elongation as against static belaying

Maximum impact force during belaying

12 kN
Static belaying

6 kN   4 kN   2,5 kN

Dynamic belaying

the relatively small increase in the fall length must be accepted because of the reduction of the forces in the entire belay chain.

Impact force, braking force, fall energy

The impact force is defined as the maximum force developed in the rope when a falling climber is held. If a climber has fallen the free fall height, the rope begins to stretch and generates an increasing force which delays the fall affects on the falling body until the value of the braking force of the dynamic belay methods is reached. Afterwards the rope runs, with approximately constant braking force, through the braking device until the fall energy has been totally absorbed through braking and rope extension. In the case of runners part of the fall energy is also absorbed by rope friction at rock and ice edges. Thus the fall energy is absorbed by various components of the entire belay system, as detailed below:

- by the rope through stretching
- by the braking device through rope friction
- by runners through rope friction in the karabiner
- by rock and ice edges through rope friction

- by slings at the runners through stretching
- by rope knots through tightening
- and to a lesser extent by other factors of less significance

The more components involved in absorbing the fall energy - especially the runners - the less the braking device is brought to play and the less rope run-through will occur. This can go so far, that the rope does not slip at all, thus the belay becomes effectively a static one. All the energy of the fall is then absorbed by the other components. This situation usually occurs in the case of a low fall factor. The belayer may then not experience any force at all.

If the rope run through occurs at the braking device, the belay becomes dynamic. The force developed then rises to its limit.

Rope run through and impact force extension
In the case of a dynamic belay the rope slides through the braking device in a controlled manner for a certain length. The more fall energy needing to be absorbed, and the lower the characteristic

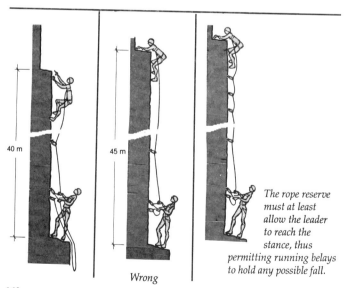

40 m

45 m

Wrong

The rope reserve must at least allow the leader to reach the stance, thus permitting running belays to hold any possible fall.

braking force of the belay method, the longer will be the rope run-through.

The rope stretches due to the braking force and, if appropriate, due to the impact force in the rope. This is called the impact force extension.

The fall factor and the impact force
In all situations, when a fall occurs, the rope absorbs fall energy by stretching. If a lot of rope is available to hold a fall, then there will be a lot of rope stretch, the consequence of which is a low impact force. If, on the other hand, only a short rope is available, it also can stretch only little, which leads to a higher impact force. This ratio of the fall height to the amount of rope paid out is called the fall factor:

$$\text{Fall factor} = \frac{\text{fall height in metres}}{\text{the given out rope length in metres}} \quad \text{(no units)}$$

As the applied force on the braking device approaches its characteristic braking force, the rope starts to slide through, and the belay becomes dynamic. The HMS goes dynamic with a fall factor of about 0.8.

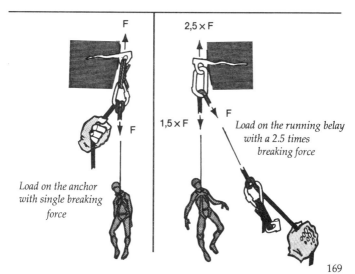

Load on the anchor with single breaking force

Load on the running belay with a 2.5 times breaking force

Which belay method to choose?

Three points show the distinct advantages of the HMS/Italian hitch belay, when compared with all other belay methods known until now:

- the lower the characteristic braking force, the better for the loading on the belay chain. However, this relationship cannot be extended indefinitely. The reduction is limited because of the amount of rope available for braking (also because of limits in the rope extension due to the fall). It must therefore be optimised between the effects of the braking force and the necessary braking reserve as well as the extension due to the fall. The characteristic braking force of the (chosen) belay method must range from 2 to 4 kN (approximately from 200 to 400 kgf).

- In the event of a fall, assume that the anchor point at the stance is loaded with an impact force = 1. The falling climber, on the other hand, is exposed to an impact force of 1.5 because of the rope friction in the karabiner. The load on the runner is the resultant of both forces, which means an impact force of up to 2.5(!). Consequently, in the case of an applied force in an upward direction (through a runner) the characteristic braking force should be lower than in the case of a downward direction. This variation of the characteristic braking force should adjust automatically (without the effort of the belayer), as any additional manipulation at the stance can only be obstructive. Moreover, in unexpected situations, when danger suddenly crops up, an individual is capable of reflex reactions only, not of reacting in a controlled manner.

- An optimum belaying method must function only through reflex reactions of the belayer. Other belaying methods usually require further actions on the part of the belayer (such as pulling the hand up), such actions go beyond the purely reflex reactions. Those methods have often failed in practice.

All the above requirements are met only by the HMS/Italian hitch belay.

Belaying on the body or on a fixed point

In practice, the body of the belayer cannot absorb any fall energy. Even small forces (see the sketch) cause the belayer to be pulled in the direction of the applied force. As a rule, the impact forces are far higher than those indicated and there is always the danger of injuries to the belayer through being pulled from the stance. In addition, there is another problem for the belayer, when carrying out the necessary braking action (clasping the rope with the braking hand). To optimise the survival

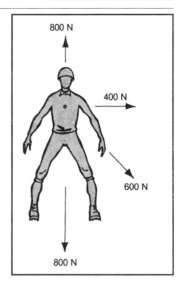

of the whole roped party, avoid belaying at an anchor point too close to the (belayer's) body.

Forces and braking during a fall into a crevasse

On a glacier, the whole roped party is moving together, thus the forces and braking operation in the event of a fall into a crevasse, is different from that in the event of a fall on rock.

As soon as the falling climber disappears into the crevasse, the rope immediately comes under load. The force applied to the next person on the rope ranges from 1.5 to 2 kN (approximately 150 to 200 kgf). With a force ranging from 200 to 500 N (about 20 to 50 kgf), the effect of which is either horizontal or vertical, everybody will be dragged from their feet. Thus the next person (on the rope) is unable to stop the fall into the crevasse and is dragged to the ground (danger of injuries, bone fractures, dislocation). The same happens in most cases to the third member of the roped party.

Those dragged to the ground are pulled along towards the crevasse edge, until the fall energy (weight of the falling climber multiplied by the fall height) has been absorbed by friction between the rope and the crevasse edge as well as by friction between the bodies of those dragged to the ground and the surface of the glacier (at any given time the friction force multiplied by braking length). Even when the fall into the crevasse has been stopped, the climber dragged to the ground is still under the effect of a force of approximately 500 N (about 50 kgf).

If the braking effect is insufficient and the crevasse deep enough, the leader may be followed into the crevasse by other members of the party.

Concluding observations

During recent years much has been done in the field of alpine safety. The equipment has been improved to an extent never previously envisaged, so that safety techniques have been optimised, and the fear of mountains has been replaced by more positive views.

However, we must not deceive ourselves: the mountains are as dangerous as ever and human beings are still as prone to inadequacies. According to statistics, about 80 per cent of all alpine accidents can be attributed to human error; hence climbers have only themselves to blame.

It is hoped that everything in this book about equipment, techniques and safety will contribute towards a reduction in the number of avoidable accidents. A considerable number of accidents still remain which cannot be avoided and for which "fate or destiny" have to be blamed.

CICERONE GUIDES

Cicerone publish a wide range of reliable guides to walking and climbing in Europe

FRANCE
TOUR OF MONT BLANC
CHAMONIX MONT BLANC - A Walking Guide
TOUR OF THE OISANS: GR54
WALKING THE FRENCH ALPS: GR5
THE CORSICAN HIGH LEVEL ROUTE: GR20
THE WAY OF ST JAMES: GR65
THE PYRENEAN TRAIL: GR10
TOUR OF THE QUEYRAS
ROCK CLIMBS IN THE VERDON

FRANCE / SPAIN
WALKS AND CLIMBS IN THE PYRENEES
ROCK CLIMBS IN THE PYRENEES

SPAIN
WALKS & CLIMBS IN THE PICOS DE EUROPA
WALKING IN MALLORCA
BIRDWATCHING IN MALLORCA
COSTA BLANCA CLIMBS

FRANCE / SWITZERLAND
THE JURA - Walking the High Route and Winter Ski Traverses
CHAMONIX TO ZERMATT The Walker's Haute Route

SWITZERLAND
WALKS IN THE ENGADINE
THE VALAIS - A Walking Guide
THE ALPINE PASS ROUTE

GERMANY / AUSTRIA
THE KALKALPEN TRAVERSE
KLETTERSTEIG - Scrambles
WALKING IN THE BLACK FOREST
MOUNTAIN WALKING IN AUSTRIA
WALKING IN THE SALZKAMMERGUT
KING LUDWIG WAY

ITALY
ALTA VIA - High Level Walks in the Dolomites
VIA FERRATA - Scrambles in the Dolomites
ITALIAN ROCK - Selected Rock Climbs in Northern Italy
CLASSIC CLIMBS IN THE DOLOMITES
WALKING IN THE DOLOMITES

OTHER AREAS
THE MOUNTAINS OF GREECE - A Walker's Guide
CRETE: Off the beaten track
Treks & Climbs in the mountains of RHUM & PETRA, JORDAN
THE ATLAS MOUNTAINS

GENERAL OUTDOOR BOOKS
LANDSCAPE PHOTOGRAPHY
FIRST AID FOR HILLWALKERS
MOUNTAIN WEATHER
MOUNTAINEERING LITERATURE
THE ADVENTURE ALTERNATIVE

CANOEING
SNOWDONIA WILD WATER, SEA & SURF
WILDWATER CANOEING
CANOEIST'S GUIDE TO THE NORTH EAST

CARTOON BOOKS
ON FOOT & FINGER
ON MORE FEET & FINGERS
LAUGHS ALONG THE PENNINE WAY

(ᵖ) **CICERONE PRESS**

Also a full range of guidebooks to walking, scrambling, ice-climbing, rock climbing, and other adventurous pursuits in Britain and abroad

*Other guides are constantly being added to the Cicerone List.
Available from bookshops, outdoor equipment shops or direct (send for price list)
from CICERONE, 2 POLICE SQUARE, MILNTHORPE, CUMBRIA, LA7 7PY*

CICERONE GUIDES

Cicerone publish a wide range of reliable guides to walking and climbing in Britain - and other general interest books

LAKE DISTRICT - General Books
LAKELAND VILLAGES
WORDSWORTH'S DUDDON REVISITED
THE REGATTA MEN
REFLECTIONS ON THE LAKES
OUR CUMBRIA
PETTIE
THE HIGH FELLS OF LAKELAND
CONISTON COPPER A History
LAKELAND - A taste to remember (Recipes)
THE LOST RESORT?
CHRONICLES OF MILNTHORPE
LOST LANCASHIRE

LAKE DISTRICT - Guide Books
CASTLES IN CUMBRIA
WESTMORLAND HERITAGE WALK
IN SEARCH OF WESTMORLAND
CONISTON COPPER MINES
SCRAMBLES IN THE LAKE DISTRICT
MORE SCRAMBLES IN THE LAKE DISTRICT
WINTER CLIMBS IN THE LAKE DISTRICT
WALKS IN SILVERDALE/ARNSIDE
BIRDS OF MORECAMBE BAY
THE EDEN WAY

NORTHERN ENGLAND (outside the Lakes
THE YORKSHIRE DALES A walker's guide
WALKING IN THE SOUTH PENNINES
LAUGHS ALONG THE PENNINE WAY
WALKS IN THE YORKSHIRE DALES (3 VOL)
WALKS TO YORKSHIRE WATERFALLS
NORTH YORK MOORS Walks
THE CLEVELAND WAY & MISSING LINK
DOUGLAS VALLEY WAY
THE RIBBLE WAY
WALKING NORTHERN RAILWAYS EAST
WALKING NORTHERN RAILWAYS WEST
HERITAGE TRAILS IN NW ENGLAND
BIRDWATCHING ON MERSEYSIDE
THE LANCASTER CANAL
FIELD EXCURSIONS IN NW ENGLAND
ROCK CLIMBS LANCASHIRE & NW
THE ISLE OF MAN COASTAL PATH

DERBYSHIRE & EAST MIDLANDS
WHITE PEAK WALKS - 2 Vols
HIGH PEAK WALKS
WHITE PEAK WAY
KINDER LOG
THE VIKING WAY
THE DEVIL'S MILL (Novel)
WHISTLING CLOUGH (Novel)
WALES & WEST MIDLANDS
THE RIDGES OF SNOWDONIA
HILLWALKING IN SNOWDONIA
ASCENT OF SNOWDON
WELSH WINTER CLIMBS
SNOWDONIA WHITE WATER SEA & SURF
SCRAMBLES IN SNOWDONIA
ROCK CLIMBS IN WEST MIDLANDS
THE SHROPSHIRE HILLS A Walker's Guide

SOUTH & SOUTH WEST ENGLAND
WALKS IN KENT
THE WEALDWAY & VANGUARD WAY
SOUTH DOWNS WAY & DOWNS LINK
COTSWOLD WAY
WALKING ON DARTMOOR
SOUTH WEST WAY - 2 Vol

SCOTLAND
SCRAMBLES IN LOCHABER
SCRAMBLES IN SKYE
THE ISLAND OF RHUM
CAIRNGORMS WINTER CLIMBS
WINTER CLIMBS BEN NEVIS & GLENCOE
SCOTTISH RAILWAY WALKS
TORRIDON A Walker's Guide
SKI TOURING IN SCOTLAND

THE MOUNTAINS OF ENGLAND & WALES
VOL 1 WALES
VOL 2 ENGLAND

*Also a full range of guidebooks
to walking, scrambling, ice-climbing,
rock climbing, and other adventurous
pursuits in Europe*

---

*Other guides are constantly being added to the Cicerone List.
Available from bookshops, outdoor equipment shops or direct (send for price list)
from CICERONE, 2 POLICE SQUARE, MILNTHORPE, CUMBRIA, LA7 7PY*

MOUNTAIN

Still the Definitive International Magazine for Mountaineers and Rock Climbers.

Mountain is published six times a year: January, March, May, July, September, and November and is available from specialist retailers throughout Britain and the world. Subscriptions and back issues are available from Mountain Magazine Limited, Globe Works, Penistone Rd., Sheffield, S6 3AE.
Tel: 0742-922340 Fax: 0742-820016

IF YOU LIKE ADVENTUROUS ACTIVITIES ON MOUNTAINS OR HILLS YOU WILL ENJOY READING:

CLIMBER

AND HILLWALKER

MOUNTAINEERING/HILLWALKING/TREKKING ROCK CLIMBING/SCRAMBLING IN BRITAIN AND ABROAD

AVAILABLE FROM NEWSAGENTS, OUTDOOR EQUIPMENT SHOPS, OR BY SUBSCRIPTION (6-12 MONTHS) FROM OUTRAM MAGAZINES, THE PLAZA TOWER, EAST KILBRIDE, GLASGOW G74 1LW

THE WALKERS' MAGAZINE

the great OUTDOORS

COMPULSIVE MONTHLY READING FOR ANYONE INTERESTED IN WALKING

AVAILABLE FROM NEWSAGENTS, OUTDOOR EQUIPMENT SHOPS, OR BY SUBSCRIPTION (6-12 MONTHS) FROM OUTRAM MAGAZINES, THE PLAZA TOWER, EAST KILBRIDE, GLASGOW G74 1LW

Printed in Gt. Britain by
CARNMOR PRINT & DESIGN
95-97 LONDON RD. PRESTON